Extending Lending

Extending Lending
The Case for a State-backed Investment Bank

David Merlin-Jones

Civitas: Institute for the Study of Civil Society
London

First Published February 2012

© Civitas 2012
55 Tufton Street
London SW1P 3QL

email: books@civitas.org.uk

All rights reserved

ISBN 978-1-906837-36-5

Independence: Civitas: Institute for the Study of Civil Society is a registered educational charity (No. 1085494) and a company limited by guarantee (No. 04023541). Civitas is financed from a variety of private sources to avoid over-reliance on any single or small group of donors.

All publications are independently refereed. All the Institute's publications seek to further its objective of promoting the advancement of learning. The views expressed are those of the authors, not of the Institute.

Typeset by
Civitas

Printed in Great Britain by
Berforts Group Ltd
Stevenage SG1 2BH

A bank is a place that will lend you money if you can prove that you don't need it.

Bob Hope

Contents

	Page
Author	viii
Acknowledgements	viii
Foreword	ix
Preface	xv
Summary	xviii
Introduction: A Hypothetical Case	1

Part One: Existing Models

1 The Industrial and Commercial Finance Corporation	7
2 The US Small Business Administration	26
3 KfW	50

Part Two: The Model of the Enterprise Bank

4 Existing British Institutions Aimed at Alleviating The Macmillan Gap	71
5 What Should the Enterprise Bank Do?	77
6 How the Enterprise Bank Should Operate	86
7 How the Enterprise Bank Should Be Funded	100
8 Conclusion	105
Notes	107

Author

David Merlin-Jones is Director of the Wealth of Nations Project at Civitas. He is a graduate from Exeter College, University of Oxford where he studied History. He joined Civitas in 2010 as a Research Fellow, focusing on economic issues and, in particular, British manufacturing and energy. He has previously authored $CO_{2.1}$: *Beyond the EU's Emission Trading System* (2012) and *Chain Reactions: How the chemical industry can shrink our carbon footprint* (2011). He has published other Civitas reports including *Rock Solid? An investigation into the British cement industry* (2010) and co-authored (with David G. Green) *A Strategy for Economic Growth* (2011). His work has been discussed on the BBC and in the *Financial Times, The Sunday Times* and *Telegraph* amongst others.

Merlin-Jones originally approached the subject of bank reform and the need for a state-backed investment bank in *The Industrial and Commercial Finance Corporation: lessons from the past for the future*, published October 2010. This report has been reproduced here with slight changes as Chapter 1.

Acknowledgements:

Special thanks to Lucy Hatton, researcher at Civitas, who assisted in the creation of this report and wrote the chapter on KfW.

Foreword

We need a state-funded Enterprise Bank for two main reasons. First, it is widely accepted that we need to rebalance the economy in favour of manufacturing, but it is not within the means of the private sector to undertake the massive re-investment that is required. In particular, the banks are still fragile and under international pressure to re-capitalise. They can't build up their reserves and step up lending simultaneously. A state-financed Enterprise Bank is the only solution that can be introduced rapidly.

Second, quite apart from the urgency of our current economic situation, there is a public interest in some state funding of productive enterprise. Financial institutions will judge projects by the size of the return on their investment, but a new factory will benefit many others besides the investor. It will benefit employees and there will be a rebound effect on the local area, where the additional incomes and demand for services and supplies will stimulate economic activity. Because the public benefit is not captured by the return to the investor, it can convincingly be argued that private investors will tend to under-invest. The acknowledged existence of a wider public benefit is why so many economically successful countries subsidise loans to private enterprise, especially small businesses.

It is, perhaps, not surprising that Germany—with its 'social market' tradition—has a very successful state investment bank, KfW, but few people are aware of the scale on which the American government subsidises loans to business. Since the 1950s the Small Business Administration (SBA) has supplied 20 million small businesses with financial help by supporting them when commercial banks would not. It does not make loans direct to customers, but guarantees private loans against default, a subsidy that vastly increases the availability of private finance. Some of America's largest banks are among the most active in the system. The two largest loan issuers in 2010 were Wells Fargo Bank ($476m) and JP Morgan Chase Bank ($229). At present, the SBA has about 219,000 loans on its books, worth around $45 billion, making it the largest investor in US businesses.

Nonetheless, there are many critics of state investment banks. What are their chief arguments? The underlying assumption is that markets allocate capital efficiently and that state subsidies will interfere with the process. Some say that crony capitalism will result. Money will go to companies with good political connections, not sound commercial projects; or party-political interests will determine investments, leading to the propping up of lame-duck industries in marginal seats; or vanity projects named after political leaders will multiply. Moreover, according to the critics, governments can't pick winners. If civil servants rather than elected politicians make decisions, they are likely to invest badly because they don't bear the risk of failure. Entrepreneurs, by comparison, will invest more wisely because they stand to lose everything.

How true is the claim that financial institutions allocate capital efficiently? The recent banking crisis has perhaps shattered for ever the image of banks as wise investors.

The government-appointed Independent Commission on Banking, chaired by Sir John Vickers, reported in 2011 that banks faced 'misaligned incentives' that had led them to compete 'by lowering lending standards'. The Commission aimed to encourage banks to compete 'to serve

FOREWORD

customers well rather than exploiting lack of customer awareness or poor regulation'.[1] Far from allocating capital efficiently, the report said that: 'the inflation of leverage in the past decade led to recession, not growth'.[2] It found competition could be a 'weak and/or a mixed blessing' and have damaging side-effects, such as 'financial system risk created by lax and under-capitalised lending'.[3]

The Future of Banking Commission (FBC), set up by the Consumers Association, reported in 2010 and shared the concerns of the Vickers commission. The FBC concluded that banks focused too narrowly on the short-term interest of shareholders: 'our financial system can often encourage short-term behaviour in companies, which is often against the long-term shareholder interest'.[4] For example, one common measure of performance was return on equity (ROE), the annual profit as a percentage of equity capital. According to Professor Jon Danielsson of the London School of Economics: it was 'straightforward for any trader or financial institution to manipulate the risk measurement... indeed this is one reason why so many banks lost so much money in the crisis. They were measuring risk incorrectly, in no small measure because they were gaming the system to extremes.'[5]

The commission gave the example of RBS between 2004 and 2007, when its performance looked impressive. Executives were remunerated with annual bonuses based on 'operating profit, earnings per share and return on equity'. The ROE of the bank varied from 17.5 per cent to 18.7 per cent and in 2007 executives received annual bonuses of up to 220 per cent of annual salary, ranging from £1.4m to £2.6m.[6] However, as we were to learn later, the rate had been achieved by taking on more debts and additional risks that eventually destroyed the company.

At the beginning of the period, its assets (loans) were 16.9 times its equity capital and, at the end, 25.6 times. The return on assets fell from 0.94 per cent to 0.65 per cent but executives were rewarded for increasing the bank's ROE.

The FBC accepted that many publicly listed companies (not only banks) whose shares were widely held had become 'ownerless corporations', which allowed their executives to run banks in their own interests. The problem has been particularly important for banks because the search for short-term profit generated huge losses that fell on the taxpayer. Many companies were owned by long-term shareholders like pension funds that might have been expected to seek enduring returns and avoid financial chicanery. However, in practice they were represented by fund managers who encouraged banks to borrow and lend more, with the intention of maximising short-term returns. Stephen Green, the group chairman of HSBC, told the Commission that fund managers would ask 'why we weren't gearing ourselves up more, why we weren't buying shares back, why we weren't realising certain assets where the book value was substantially below the market value—all of [which was] rather short-termist in its focus'.[7] Gaming the system to maximise the bonuses that executives could extract had become the norm—a very far cry from the efficient allocation of capital.

Worse still, banks were receiving a public subsidy that encouraged them to place risky bets. Andrew Haldane, Executive Director for Financial Stability at the Bank of England, has estimated the reduction in funding costs arising from the perceived 'too big to fail' subsidy for the top five UK banks between 2007 and 2009. He calculated that it was worth over £50 billion per year on average, roughly equivalent to annual profits for those banks at the time.

Despite these structural problems being revealed and widely discussed, they have not yet been resolved, despite the Vickers Report and a number of international initiatives. An alternative is therefore necessary, but it is important that obvious pitfalls are avoided. For this reason, David Merlin-Jones describes Britain's experience of an earlier industry bank, the Industrial and Commercial Finance Corporation, and two overseas examples, Germany's KfW and America's Small Business Administration.

Finally, Merlin-Jones considers how to finance the proposed Enterprise Bank. The quickest method would be for the Bank of England to invent about £10 billion under its quantitative easing programme and buy bonds in the Enterprise Bank. Other bonds could be sold on the open market, in the same way that treasury bonds are currently marketed. Terms of ten years at the going interest rate would be fitting. It would not be advisable to sell voting shares because it is too easy for control to fall into the hands of small groups with a different agenda, quite possibly merely to maximise the amount they can personally extract from the venture.

The Enterprise Bank's method of operation should be like that of KfW. It should aim to supplement, not displace, competing private banks. We propose an institution that operates in three main ways. First, like America's SBA, it should give guarantees for private loans, thus increasing the private funds available to SMEs. The Enterprise Bank's funds would only be called upon in the event of default. Second, it could supplement private loans, perhaps by matching them 50:50. In such cases loans would be administered through commercial banks for a fee. Third, the Enterprise Bank should operate an independent loans programme, funded 100 per cent from its own resources. Loan applications should be appraised by the Enterprise Bank's own experts, but administered through commercial banks for a fee.

David G. Green

Preface

The facts:

- Thirty-five per cent of small and medium-sized businesses sought finance in 2007. This rose to 42 per cent in 2010.
- For those seeking loan finance, around three-quarters of businesses approached banks.
- In 2007, successful loan finance approaches to banks were around 90 per cent. This fell to 65 per cent in 2010.
- Five out of every six businesses that expect to need future finance anticipate seeking it from banks.

Britain faces its worst economic crisis since the Great Depression. Small and medium sized enterprises (SMEs) are being starved of funds because they do not fit in with commercial lenders' priorities. Despite the backlash to the Great Recession of 2008-09 and the Vickers Report, little has been done to combat the short-termism of private sector lending. Moreover, banks are under pressure to recapitalise, which has pushed up the cost of borrowing. The announcement of £20 billion's worth of loan guarantees in the Chancellor's November 2011 Autumn Statement is a step in the right direction, but not a lasting one.

A permanent solution to the 'equity gap' is needed and for this Britain needs a state-backed investment bank geared to doing everything the commercial banks are unwilling to do for SMEs. This institution is labelled within this report 'the Enterprise Bank'. It will aim to improve the state of the UK economy, providing funds so that companies can expand, offer more jobs and export more. Supporting the most enterprising companies who take risks but offer potentially great rewards will be at the heart of its role. It will invest in and lend to *any* company that can prove it is a commercially viable business that will benefit from the funding, regardless of sector or political value. It will be run as a viable business and for a profit, although not to the same extent as in the private sector. It will be a real bank, simply offering more favourable rates where possible and significantly extended repayment periods. It will cooperate with and augment the private sector.

We need this Enterprise Bank (EB) now. It will be of little consolation to the businesses already starved of funds if the EB is set up in two or five years' time, by which point many will have ceased to exist. Instead, the government must be bold and not find itself embroiled in a distracting argument about the value of the free market versus state intervention. The EB is about supplementing the free market and filling in holes, not displacing it. It is a pragmatic institution which will resonate across the political spectrum. This consensus exists because it is known just what a pressing matter reviving the British economy is.

This report looks at three major state-backed investment mechanisms from the past and present as examples of how the EB could be run and what it could concentrate on doing.

- The defunct Industrial and Commercial Finance Corporation (ICFC) was an obvious choice. As an historical British institution, it proves that the UK does have the ability to produce a very successful industrial bank that challenges the commercial lenders on their own terms. As well as finance, it also provided borrowers with industrial expertise. Its eventual transformation into Investors in Industry (3i) also demonstrates how not to provide the EB with funding.

- The Kreditanstalt für Wiederaufbau, now known just as KfW, is a clear European example of a successful state-backed investment bank and a lesson Britain should be keen to learn from. Via shrewd investment based on economic priorities, it was single-handedly the most important tool that first revived Western Germany from World War II, then Eastern Germany after Reunification.

- The American Small Business Administration (SBA) is a counterpoint to the previous two examples, investing indirectly in American SMEs. It demonstrates that even in the country least associated with industrial planning, the government is attentive to the economic value and needs of small businesses. If the pre-eminent home of capitalism can be rigorously pragmatic, why can't Britain?

Learning the lessons of these experiences, the blueprint for the EB can be created. It is possible to see from these that while the Green Investment Bank (GIB) will be constructed with good intentions, it is not the enterprise bank the economy actually needs and will not deliver the hoped-for industrial renaissance, green or not, that it promises. However, its creation proves that support for a state-backed investment institution exists. To kick-start the economy, there can be no favouritism and no compromises.

Summary

- Small and medium-sized enterprises (SMEs) in Britain are being starved of funding due to the short-termism of private sector lending, and little is being done to combat this.

- The answer to the equity gap is a state-backed 'Enterprise Bank' which will support enterprising, risk-taking companies that offer great rewards. It will be a real bank offering more favourable rates and longer lengths of repayment to viable businesses.

- In Britain today, in contrast to Germany and the US, there is no alternative option for a small business owner to obtain finance if commercial lenders do not deem the provision of funding to be worth the risks involved with small, long-term loans.

The Industrial and Commercial Finance Corporation in the UK

- The ICFC was created in Britain in 1945 in response to the Macmillan Committee's report of 1931 which identified a sizeable 'gap' in funding for SMEs, which became known as the Macmillan Gap. The ICFC provided funding of between £5,000 and £200,000.

- The ICFC determined the price of a loan on the basis of the applicant business's future potential, and their past success. This proved to be an effective method of evaluation that could be built upon by the Enterprise Bank.

- The ICFC had a contentious relationship with most commercial banks, which were forced to fund it, and failed effectively to refer businesses to the ICFC when they were unwilling to help.

- The ICFC had a decentralised, regional structure which enabled it to provide localised expertise to its customers. Such localisation ensured regional conditions were taken into consideration.

- In the 1970s, the ICFC began to lose its identity and purpose, as it was merged with the FCI to become Finance for Industry and later 3i. The remit of this new group differed from that of the ICFC and mergers and acquisitions increasingly became its mainstay.

The Small Business Administration in the US

- The SBA is a national investment institution in the US that, unlike the ICFC, has managed mostly to retain its original form and aims over the last 60 years. Since its inception it has supplied approximately 20 million SMEs with financial assistance.

- The SBA does not directly provide loans itself, but provides guarantees on loans provided by various lenders that have signed up to its guidelines. SBA-backed loans are for longer terms, have lower repayments and require less collateral than those offered by standard commercial lenders.

- Due to repeated expansions of the availability of funds through the SBA programmes and the introduction of new programmes, SMEs in the US were able successfully to weather the effects of the 2008-09 recession.

- The SBA is considerably constrained by the actions of commercial banks, as the latter must channel the request from the potential borrower on to the SBA.

- Evidence also suggests that as the majority of SBA customers are micro-businesses of less than five employees, SBA-backed funds are being used merely to keep these businesses afloat rather than allowing them to expand, and questions are raised as to whether resources should be focused on maintaining existing jobs or providing new ones.

KfW in Germany

- KfW was set up post-war to support the reconstruction of Germany. It is owned 80 per cent by the German Federal Government, and 20 per cent by the German Federal States. Consequently the loans and bonds it offers in assistance for German businesses are considered commitments of the Federal Republic.

- KfW today has several separate arms, each with their own objectives, and the priorities it pursues are substantially broader than its initial purpose. The wide-ranging priorities of KfW demonstrate that one state-backed institution can focus on a variety of objectives and be successful at achieving them all.

- Despite its significant losses of 2007 & 2008, the financial crisis proved KfW's aptitude for supporting Germany's SMEs. The SME sector effectively weathered the crisis and, by introducing a series of new loan programmes as instructed by the Federal Government's economic stimulus packages, KfW contributed to not only the maintenance of existing jobs but the creation of new ones.

- KfW's long-standing programme of export financing for German companies has both encouraged domestic economic growth and also the industrial development of developing countries.

The aims of the Enterprise Bank model

- There are three main roles that the Enterprise Bank (EB) should take on: funding SMEs, mitigating risk and providing advice. The three are linked and together are essential for the EB to reach its potential.

- It should aim to fill the present equity gap, of between £250,000-£500,000 and £2-3 million.

- The EB's decision-making framework should be similar to the ICFC's and grant funding based on the opinions of industrial experts.

- By providing expert advice to the borrower, the EB can also reduce some of the risk involved in financing. The cost of this advice could be payable with a slightly higher interest rate on the loan, for example.

- The EB could also take heed of the role that KfW and the SBA play in monitoring and reporting on the SME sector in their respective countries. In this way the EB can become a voice for SMEs in relations with the government and provide a regular report on the current situation with regard to small business in the UK.

How the Enterprise Bank should operate

- The relationship between the EB and commercial banks should be two-tiered. If the private sector will not grant a loan, then a company would apply for an EB loan through a commercial bank in the first instance and, if unsuccessful there, subsequently apply directly to the EB.

- There would be a financial incentive for commercial banks to administer EB loans in the form of a fee.
- The two-tier structure will ensure that, if commercial banks are complacent and uninterested in providing finance through the EB, SMEs will not suffer as they are able to approach the EB directly for an assessment of viability.
- The easiest way to set up the EB would be to use RBS, an existing state-owned institution that has experience in providing funding, and has the staff and infrastructure that would be required.
- The EB would be politically independent and attempt to reinstate the personal relationship between bank manager and customer, in order to ensure that acceptance or rejection of a loan application is not based on merely arbitrary criteria.
- The EB would necessarily have a decentralised organisational structure, and not be based in London, which is very far from most manufacturers in the UK.

How the Enterprise Bank should be funded

- Following the initial injection from the government, the EB should be able to continue to fund itself through activity on the capital markets, as does KfW and the European Investment Bank.
- Redirecting some of the funds provided through quantitative easing into the EB is a possible source of funds. Further possibilities include inviting commercial banks to invest.

Introduction:
A Hypothetical Case Study

It is best to begin with a story, set in Britain, the US and Germany. In all three countries, there is an identical, hypothetical manufacturer of widgets who has been very successful since he started up his small business ten years ago, employing half a dozen people. Since then, demand for his widgets has soared as his reputation for quality has spread. Our manufacturer reinvested the initial profits in hiring more staff, now up to a dozen, and small capital investments to streamline the process. He has now reached maximum capacity of production and has started to turn down orders that cannot be met. Without investing in a much larger widget-making machine, that will double capacity, he is stuck. This machine is a very large investment, and it would take too long to build up a reserve of funds from profits to buy it, so he decides to apply to his bank for a loan to purchase it. It is here that the stories of the three countries begin to diverge.

In Britain, the story ends all too soon. The manufacturer approaches the big commercial bank he has been banking with for ten years. The bank, for whatever reason, has decided that widget making is a risky sector to lend to at present, and therefore rejects his loan application. The manufacturer protests, and highlights his consistent commercial success, delivering profits every quarter after the initial start-up of the business despite the recession. He also points out his full order books and the long-term demand for widgets. The bank manager acknowledges that his is a very successful small business and is creditworthy, but that there is still nothing they can do, because head-office policy is that no widget sector investments can be made. Our manufacturer is forced to leave empty handed. There is nowhere else he can turn, and as he is not willing to sell equity in the company and diminish his control over it, he decides to simply continue with business as usual and turn down the orders he cannot deliver.

If the bank is able to offer the manufacturer a loan under the Enterprise Finance Guarantee (EFG) scheme, provided the sole reason for his initial rejection is a lack of collateral, it may still be able to grant him a loan. If the bank is able to do so, and decides it is willing, it could finance up to £1 million for the new machine, with a 75 per cent government guarantee so that its risk is reduced. However, the EFG scheme might not be of any help to the manufacturer as there are still some risks involved for the bank. The new National Loan Guarantee Scheme might also be of help, allowing banks to raise funds in wholesale money markets and pass on the cost saving to businesses. However, this still relies on the bank being willing to supply the loan in the first place.

In America, the story ends more positively. As before, the commercial bank refuses to grant our manufacturer a loan outright, but is quick to suggest that he applies to the bank for a Small Business Administration (SBA) backed loan, designed to help exactly his sort of business. He applies for a type 7(a) loan, specifically designed for the expansion of existing businesses. The bank ensures he is creditworthy and meets SBA eligibility criteria and then grants him a loan, backed 75 per cent by the SBA because it is over $150,000. Repayment is to be over ten years, so the loan has a higher interest rate than commercial loans and some shorter SBA-backed loans. However, because the manufacturer looked quite safe, the end rate was still

INTRODUCTION: A HYPOTHETICAL CASE STUDY

competitive and pleased both parties. The manufacturer purchases the machinery, expands production to meet demand and goes on to hire a few more workers.

In Germany, there is a similar ending. The commercial bank still refuses to grant the loan but it proposes that the manufacturer apply for a loan from state-backed KfW. Indeed, the manufacturer can approach the commercial bank for an application to KfW without even needing to be rejected. The commercial bank assists the manufacturer in completing the application form for the loan, and decides whether or not to grant it. The loan comes from KfW and the commercial bank's role from then on is merely as administrator. As the company has been in existence for more than three years, the manufacturer applies for a KfW Entrepreneur loan to cover the cost of the machinery. With this loan, KfW, and effectively the Federal Government, takes on 50 per cent of the indemnity, reducing the risk of lending for the commercial bank and encouraging it to support the financing of the new widget-making machine. Being an SME, the manufacturer also receives reductions on the ten-year fixed-interest rate for the loan and, having decided to repay it over ten years, is entitled to a two-year grace period in which he need only pay the interest. The manufacturer is very pleased with this as he will be able to increase his revenue with the new machine before he must make repayments. The bank is also much less likely to see repayments missed. Like with the American example, jobs and profits increase as a result.

In these three stories then, it is the British one that is the odd one out. If commercial lenders refuse to play ball, then there is no alternative that does not involve the surrender of equity, and many SMEs would rather stagnate than give this up. This private problem is so large that it is a public problem for the UK; public, because the nation as a whole is losing out on the growth of these SMEs that would lead to greater employment, larger profits, more exports and increased tax returns.

Part One
Existing Models

1

The Industrial and Commercial Finance Corporation

Introduction

The Industrial and Commercial Finance Corporation (ICFC) was created in 1945 as the result of a political decision to increase the availability of funding to small and medium sized enterprises (SMEs). Its creation was a reaction to the findings of the Macmillan Committee's report of 1931 which realised: 'there is... no recognised and readily accessible channel, corresponding to the new issue market for larger firms, through which the small industrialist can raise long-term funds'.[1] The problem became known as the 'Macmillan Gap'. The City and the Stock Exchange were focused on overseas commerce and the 'big five' banks that dominated British banking did not find raising long-term capital for SMEs sufficiently lucrative. The cost to them of providing a loan or making an equity investment of £100,000 was roughly the same as for a much larger sum. The ICFC was created in the hope of plugging the Macmillan Gap as its Memorandum of Association made clear. The company aimed: 'to provide credit... for industrial and commercial business or enterprises in Great Britain, particularly in cases where the existing facilities provided by banking institutions and the Stock Exchange are not readily or easily available'.[2] The ICFC therefore was to provide funding for loans of between £5,000 (the point at which commercial banks stopped lending) and £200,000 (the point at which lending resumed).

The ICFC was successful in partially alleviating a huge problem, but the Macmillan Gap was so wide, and demand for ICFC loans was so great, that a considerable shortfall remained. On the whole, though, the ICFC has been judged a success. The official history was written by Richard Coopey, a Fellow at the LSE, and Donald Clarke, an ex-director of 3i. The latter pointed out that the ICFC 'provided a national service at no cost to the taxpayer and a substantial return for its shareholders at minimal cost to them'.[3] By 1983 it was renamed Investors in Industry (3i) and became a private limited company focusing on buyouts rather than loans.

The Macmillan Gap remains a problem for Britain to this day, and while successive governments have tried to increase funding to SMEs through direct initiatives and quangos, these measures have rarely been as successful as the ICFC. Important lessons can be learnt from the ICFC for tackling the UK's current SME financing crisis and for the establishment of a new industry bank for Britain: the Enterprise Bank.

Initial assumptions

When the ICFC was initially created to fill the Macmillan Gap, there was still scepticism about the Corporation's basic model of targeting business that other banks would often try to avoid. Moreover, the established shareholder banks that were forced to fund the ICFC saw the model in their own terms and therefore assumed that providing long-term loans for high-risk enterprises at a low interest rate was a doomed way to practise business. This reinforced their instinctive disapproval of the ICFC's existence. This view was also apparent within the Bank of England, which felt the creation of the ICFC was a necessary evil to prevent Labour's original hopes for a national investment bank being realised. On the Corporation's birth, the Deputy Governor of the Bank said: 'I don't believe much in this body and hope and expect that they won't do much'.[4] The Bank of England opposed any plans to link the ICFC to government policy or to approach funding regionally. Such opposition was strengthened by the political drive behind the ICFC that gave rise to fears that Britain was moving towards a continental banking model, a view encouraged by the appointment of Lord Piercy, who was heavily involved in the Labour Party, as the ICFC's first chairman.

The opposition to the ICFC and the accusations of cronyism that surrounded its leaders were almost inevitable, but this was less of a hindrance to the Corporation than might be assumed. Once the model of the Corporation had been decided, it defended itself vigorously: 'neither the Government nor the Bank of England gave any directions to the Corporation. It has given no assistance to, nor conferred any privilege on the Corporation.'[5] This was very different from the German model of the state-sponsored investment bank, Kreditanstalt für Wiederaufbau (KfW), which had been set up post-war as the financial channel for the Marshall Plan (see p. 52).

It was clear in 1945, as it still is now, that the Macmillan Gap genuinely did exist and that SMEs were seeking funding. Unlike many other large institutions, the ICFC therefore experienced demand as soon as it was created. It had no start-up period of slow growth.

Methods

Importantly, the ICFC was a commercially viable operation and always aimed to be so. It stated that 'while it endeavours to keep its charges low and to offer reasonable terms, it does not provide capital at rates below the market level'.[6] The ICFC took pains to invest wisely in loans and if anything it can be criticised for being too cautious. For example, it could be argued that the ICFC went too far when it avoided all single product manufacturers, claiming that they were inherently unstable. Overall, its method of evaluating firms proved very successful: while the price of an ICFC loan was negotiated on the basis of a company's future potential, the value of the investment was determined by the firm's past success. This would be an important requirement for a new industrial bank to ensure that, unlike commercial banks, it assesses its investments on an individual basis by ascertaining the merits of each firm so that no worthy client is turned away. Sometimes the ICFC was willing to grant a 'holiday' from repayment to allow client companies to manoeuvre through the 'valley of death' period in their growth, where profit does not follow expansion straight away. Through such methods the ICFC helped to provide for each company's long-term survival and growth.

The loans provided by the ICFC were made at a fixed rate of interest. This was highly risky for the Corporation as it was not protected by the rise and fall of market conditions. In contrast, fixed rates that implied predictable annual repayments were highly beneficial to client companies. The ICFC aimed both to 'earn respectable profits'[7] and to 'act as an accelerator in the process of a firm's own capital formation' by allowing the client to reinvest their profits rather than pay them to the bank.[8] Unsurprisingly, no other banks followed the ICFC's example, especially after the interest fluctuations of the 1970s. The ICFC gradually abandoned its strategy in the 1970s and, by the time it became 3i in 1983, little evidence of the approach was left.

Another model was provided by the Finance Corporation for Industry (FCI), set up at the same time as the ICFC to provide for large companies. The FCI invested in a narrow number of industries and targeted these sectors alone. It therefore felt market downturns more keenly: large profits were followed rapidly by heavy losses while, in comparison, the ICFC gained steady but healthy returns. The FCI's comparatively poor performance was due to its sector targeting and, unlike the ICFC, it failed to judge firms on the basis of their commercial viability. For much of its existence, the FCI had at least half of its investments tied up in the steel industry.[9] The ICFC consciously tried to avoid this 'all-eggs-in-one-basket' approach and weathered downturns far more effectively as a result. In 1967, 21.4 per cent of the Corporation's investments were invested in 'engineering and electrical goods' but there was otherwise an even spread across all industries.[10] A modern comparison of the two bank models could be drawn with the Government's proposed Green Investment Bank. Like the FCI, it would be in danger of approaching investments dogmatically, focusing exclusively on green high-tech investments. A general industrial bank would be more profitable and more stable.

Relationship with the banks

The ICFC was simultaneously reliant on and damaged by the commercial banks. They were effectively forced to fund it and become shareholders (out of fear of nationalisation by the Labour Government) but initially all banks except Barclays refused to help foster the ICFC's business. For example, commercial banks didn't advertise the existence of the ICFC to clients and only referred 'hopeless cases' as well as undermining eventual ICFC offers by providing loans themselves once they learnt of an offer having being made.[11] By February 1946, there had been 430 applicants for ICFC loans but only 89 came from the commercial banks, of which half were from Barclays.[12] This meant effectively that the potential for the Corporation to be integrated into an 'organic chain' of finance was never realised.[13] This caused many teething problems for the Corporation, but also forced it to seek its own clients and evaluate their viability without external help. In the end, these problems became the key reasons for the long success of the ICFC, by forcing it to be self-sufficient. Nonetheless, there was still a need for a working relationship between the ICFC and commercial banks because firms relied on the Corporation to provide low-interest loans for long-term funding while the banks were still relied upon for short-term borrowing.

The limits of this working relationship were tested during the credit squeeze which began in 1951, when the banks still had to fund the ICFC to provide money to clients that they themselves were unable to lend to. This highlighted a problem that meant that when the peak of the squeeze occurred in 1955, the Corporation was pressured into withdrawing £1 million of business and a suspension of further lending. The ICFC itself felt it was 'being required to bear more than their fair share of successive squeezes'.[14] When squeezed, the shareholding commercial banks tried to offset their losses by reducing their funds to the ICFC. When all the banks did this, the

Corporation suffered unduly and Lord Piercy complained that he was 'fed up with being messed about'.[15]

The Radcliffe Committee, the follow-up to the Macmillan Committee, reported that 'there seems to have been from quite early years some feeling in the banks that the undertaking to provide funds was burdensome'.[16] This feeling was certainly mutual and Piercy told the Governor of the Bank of England that 'we are entitled to a proper latitude in the conduct of our business and after ten years we deserve the confidence of our shareholders'.[17] The 1959 decision to raise funds on the private market freed the Corporation from spending restraints, as it could raise as much capital as it wished on the open market and £45 million worth of stock was sold to allow engagement in greater investments. This gave the Corporation more independence through less reliance on banks, and the banks themselves were glad to be rid of the commitment they had borne. Uptake of the stocks began slowly, but rapidly became oversubscribed. However, the sudden influx of capital was too little too late and the constraint on the ICFC had a lasting effect on its growth, having stunted it for a decade. Moreover, the sudden independence and need to produce returns on stock sold meant short-term investing became a more attractive option, something increasingly apparent by the late 1970s.

A modern industry bank's relationship with commercial banks would have to be well defined and protected, and this would require a more amenable atmosphere than that in which the ICFC was created. While such a bank's lending should reflect the conditions of the market, its funding should not be overly reliant on commercial banks so as to prevent their self-interest jeopardising the success of the industry bank. The long-term presence of an industrial bank would have a desirable effect on the ethos of commercial bank lending to SMEs. Lord Piercy stated in 1960 that: 'the example of the ICFC has proved a stimulus to other institutions, large and small, to enter this field. It is possible that the ICFC has done more for the Gap by example than by its exertions.'[18] The banks had to react to the existence of the industrial bank, whose very creation was a critique of their own ability, and they therefore began to involve themselves in the previously neglected SME sector.

Relationship with customers

The success of the ICFC was highly reliant on its knowledge of the firms it was supporting. This was a two part exercise, involving collective expertise in specialised investment from the board of directors downwards, as well as familiarity with local businesses through its regional branches. This was a revolutionary method of doing business, and contemporaries noted 'no other City institution has ever thought it needed to bring such a wide range of expertise to bear on the propositions submitted by its clients'.[19] The ICFC employed its own specialists rather than relying on external advice and in the long term this was highly profitable for the Corporation as its bad debts fell to a level that never endangered profits. This was quite an achievement, given that many of its clients were 'firms with no real historical accounts, lacking security, and requiring long-term investment'.[20] Its specialised strength in assessing business proposals gave it a huge competitive edge. It proved capable of predicting the success of new companies. Moreover, those with potential were given special attention and sought out as clients. A new industry bank could only survive in the modern economic climate by following the same strategy of amassing a wealth of local expertise.

The regionalisation of the ICFC was the product of a perceived need to recreate the nineteenth century conditions of local investment that had been lost in the centralisation of investment through the London Stock Exchange.[21] The ICFC would take up the role of the locally informed investor who knew the business climate and their client well. This was done through actively attempting to decentralise the Corporation away from London through opening regional branches, the first of which opened in Birmingham in 1950 and was shortly followed by others in Manchester, Edinburgh, Leeds and Leicester, among others. The goal of decentralisation was 'going out and seeking clients on their own ground' and 'participating in local business communities'.[22] While other banks had branches with managers who knew their customers well, this was rarely combined with the level of technical expertise that the ICFC could offer. This is clearly a key policy for any new industrial bank and more critical since the advent of clustering, where companies in the same sector group together to share assets and resources. A regional policy towards investment would bring with it a diversity of industries centred in different localities. This would also strongly complement the current government aim of creating 'local enterprise partnerships' as funding could be sought at a local level. Moreover, the bank itself would gain from being able properly to assess the potential of companies on a local level with microeconomic knowledge, ensuring that it would not dismiss cases based on national rather than regional trends.

The ICFC aimed to foster a long-term relationship with its clients by acting responsibly, but also in a manner that satisfied the client. The Corporation was normally therefore a 'sleeping' investor unless something went wrong in the firm, in which case it sought to use its extensive expertise to help correct this. Otherwise, the ICFC would offer good advice when this was sought by the client. The result of the continuity of service it offered was that by 1954, of 460 new applications, 155 were from previous customers and 40 had applied more than twice.[23] This was a very different approach to that of normal banks, for whom SME investment was not their normal target and funds available for SMEs fluctuated over time.

Drift from purpose

By the 1960s, the ICFC had the potential to move away from its original remit as the vehicle to plug the Macmillan Gap. This was a two-part process, as the criteria for how many and to whom loans were given changed, and the Corporation began focusing on bigger money earners, such as mergers and acquisitions. The first major change was the acquisition of Technical Development Capital (TDC). TDC had been created in 1962 due to the desire to improve high-tech manufacturing and embodied the idea of Harold Wilson's speech on the 'white heat of the technological revolution'. By 1966, the TDC had failed to have a significant impact and the ICFC took it over. High-tech investment is often very risky and long-term and the ICFC had the financial reserves necessary. It also had the technical expertise and ethos to suit this form of investment. By 1970 the Corporation had used TDC to invest £6 million in over 100 companies.[24] A few good businesses performed well such as Oxford Instruments, but otherwise Coopey argued the TDC was 'only a moderate performer, with no real "shooting stars" in its portfolio'.[25]

The loss of the ICFC's overall identity and purpose began in the 1970s, when it merged with the FCI to form the umbrella group of Finance for Industry (FFI). When this occurred in 1973, the purpose of FFI was stated as, 'to provide medium- and long-term funds for the growth of British Industry'.[26] This had no explicit relation to the Macmillan Gap, and had greater freedom more in line with a general commercial bank remit than the specialised institution it had previously been. The transformation continued, especially after the economic slump of 1974 which led to the first yearly loss for the Corporation, announced the following year as £19.9 million.[27] To counter this, the lending policy was widened to allow the ICFC to maximise its potential but again this only served to dilute the purpose of the Corporation in the long-run. Indeed, by 1981 the next recession had forced the FFI to seek profit wherever it could be found, which was mostly in the capital restructuring of the firms most severely hit by the recession. By the 1980s, the Corporation's organisation, methods and goals were a far cry from those it had held 20 years previously. Clearly, this raises problems as to how a modern industrial bank would cope in a similar situation when economic downturns mean less demand for its services. The simplest solution would be to ensure the bank would not be tempted by profit but instead would simply weather out the crisis with as small a loss, if any, as possible. The ICFC survived the mid-1950s crisis without too much strain, whereas the commercial banks, with their traditional practices, suffered far more.

Interestingly, by the time of the 3i rebranding, the successor organisation to the TDC was given a hard time by the parent 3i group for being too radical in its approach to investment. 3i Ventures was to be run along the same lines, performing expertise-based long-term investment in high-risk advanced technology. The company failed to perform well in the short-term and, according to Coopey, this meant that, 'those elements within the 3i Group which had been alienated by what they saw as the cavalier style of 3i Ventures became more vociferous in their criticism of the division'.[28] By the late 1980s, 3i attacked its Venture wing, having become quite conservative in its investments, in ways similar to the banks it had originally been created to counter. With its maturation, a concern for its own interests began to grow and outweigh the potential national interest it had been set up to serve. A modern industry bank could not be allowed to change in shape and interests so dramatically, and should be tethered to its original purpose of providing funding, even if it is not in the company's short-term interest.

The development of the ICFC's greater focus on profit began in 1967 when it set up Industrial Mergers Ltd. This move was highly lucrative, but as Clarke admits in the official history: 'such a trend went completely against the traditional areas in which ICFC was developing its strength, the finance of small- and medium-sized businesses'.[29] He has attempted to absolve the Corporation from any blame, however, by arguing that this 'reflected the fact that a number of ICFC's customers were caught up in the merger wave'.[30] Regardless of this assertion, establishing Industrial Mergers Ltd was a large departure from the original role assigned to the ICFC. However, because the Government had no control over the activities of the Corporation, nothing could be done to bring it back in line and the trends continued until loans had become secondary to mergers and acquisitions when the company was rebranded in 1983. Ultimately the ICFC's transformation from industry to quasi-commercial bank, to its being finally fully privatised, was the result of there being no strong limit imposed on how the ICFC could spend its money and how funds were raised. As soon as shareholders began to take a stake in the Corporation, they were given an incentive to exert pressure to raise immediate returns, which jeopardised the original principles of SME funding. This raises serious questions for a modern industry bank as to how it would be funded and held to account. The most neutral manner would be to ensure that its articles of association, which since the 2006 Companies Act are now the sole constitutional document for a company, clearly specify the limits to its legitimate activities. The bank should state its intention of filling the Macmillan Gap by whichever means it feels is most appropriate, and to put this goal ahead of profit making—distinguishing it clearly from commercial banks. The articles of association would therefore allow funds to be raised in the private market, but would ensure that shareholder pressure to seek profit could not trump the main goal of filling the Macmillan Gap. While those interested in making a quick buck may lose interest in funding the ICFC due to this, more conscientious long-term investors would still be interested. This can be seen in the ICFC's experience, given it started raising its funds fourteen years after its creation, by which time the long-term loans had begun to truly fructify (hence the oversubscription to its stock). The bank would perhaps face initial difficulty with raising private capital, but using initial state funds to spark the first investments in SMEs and perhaps a state guarantee to safeguard the purchase of industry bank shares, the potential for private sector success is considerable.

Limits to success

As we have seen, the ICFC's potential was heavily restricted by the lack of cooperation from the commercial banks, but some of its own policies weakened its effectiveness. The aim of the model was to prevent overlapping with the business territory of the clearing banks which fell outside the Macmillan Gap. The ICFC stated that 'the Company will supplement but not supersede the activities of other lenders and financial institutions'.[31] One such restriction was the upper limit of £200,000 that it could loan, which did not rise with inflation and so increasingly tethered the Corporation. The self-conscious avoidance of competition was explicit in the ICFC's *aide-memoire* which explained that: 'the Company will not carry on a Banking business; its function will be the provision of medium and long-term credit'.[32] While this meant the *status quo* of banking was preserved, further benefit could have been derived by allowing greater competition with established banks. The ICFC, as it was in 1954, was deemed by ex-employee and economist Brian Tew to be 'excessively scrupulous' in its approach. The Radcliffe Committee also noted that the ICFC rejected more firms than it invested in and so made less of an inroad into filling the Macmillan Gap than had been hoped. Tew's opinion was shared by some inside the ICFC which stated in 1958 that while it had gained £3.8 million of new business that year, without restrictions it could have achieved an additional £7 million - £8 million on top of this.[33] Tew appealed for 'overlap at the seams' of the Gap to ensure that firms wanting just over the upper limit were not left without funding.[34]

By the time the company was reorganised in 1959 and restrictions were lifted, the Corporation saw a rise in the number of applicants, from 313 in 1958-59 to 392 the following year. As funding became easier to access, demand for it also rose. A modern industry bank would do well to learn from this lesson, that availability of funds has a direct effect on the demand for them. Few would apply if funds were hard to access or unlikely to be granted, so the openness of the bank must be strongly advertised along with its existence in general. As has been seen, the mere existence of the ICFC spurred the banks into providing funding to SMEs they had previously neglected. If the ICFC had competed head on, it would have incentivised this expansion further.

There was a tension between the ICFC's original remit of helping all forms of small industry and its being a commercially viable operation. The Corporation was criticised for not providing enough loans of less than £20,000 but the ICFC attempted to defend itself by arguing that it provided loans to companies 'on terms which do not offer a reward corresponding to the risk even if the venture is successful'.[35] The ICFC saw itself as serving its purpose through the sacrifice of profit, even if others did not agree. The conflicting ideals of the Corporation meant that it eventually drifted away from its original remit as it expanded and diversified investments. In particular, by the 1960s, the needs of the smallest firms were being overlooked. While the ICFC did not make a habit of investing in failing companies, the few that did fail were often given fresh investment if a new management took over and this 'recycling of worn-out companies' by the ICFC was one of its 'unsung achievements and an important element in its contribution to the economy'.[36] Provided a new industrial bank utilised technical knowledge to the full, this would be possible again.

The designers of the ICFC did not originally stick to the recommendations of the Macmillan Report, which advocated a fully empowered institution that could raise funds in the private market: 'Such a company might issue preference share capital or debentures.'[37] The ICFC did eventually take this form, but only after the hostility of commercial banks had become too much to bear. The Enterprise Bank should not seek to be so submissive to the *status quo* or trade outside the market. Rather, it should aim to become an integral component of the British financial system.

The ICFC's conscious attempt to offer investment outside of London also appears to have been less successful than could have been hoped. In 1967, 32.4 per cent of all investment was still tied up in London and the remainder was mostly concentrated in the Midlands.[38] This was despite the existence of the regional Corporation offices. The problem was always perceived as a temporary one and supposed to be the result of local clients being unaware of the ICFC's services. The legacy of the commercial banks deliberately not informing their customers of the ICFC's existence was seen as the root cause of this. The advances in communications since the advent of the internet mean these problems would be less grave for a modern industrial bank, which could reach its customer base far more effectively. That said, a pro-active policy towards advertising would still be necessary and, as unclaimed government grants have shown, the potential customer should not have to find out about the availability of funds by themselves.

Conclusion

By the time the ICFC had become 3i, its undertakings were analysed by one report as: 'like other venture funds, its main activities now involve sponsoring management buyouts and buy-ins, rather than providing "seed corn" and development capital to small enterprises, and it deals mainly with medium-sized enterprises'.[39] The evolution from a specialised and unique investment bank to a generic one was the product of overemphasising the commercial basis of the ICFC, which was given no government aid and had to accept the constraints of the commercial bank shareholders. Forcing the ICFC to survive purely on its own meant that short-term profit-making was overvalued. The only viable way to prevent this in a private sector industry model is to restrain the bank from acting outside the desired area through its articles of association, which would clearly define the limits of its influence and methods. Had the ICFC been established on this basis, it could have raised private sector capital (as it did from 1959), whilst avoiding being drawn into mergers and acquisitions.

In the UK, a new state-backed investment bank should combine the best elements of the private company and state institution. It could initially be set up using state funds, to begin the process of securing a positive track record that would entice private investment. The funds for such a launch are already in existence in government schemes designed for SMEs. The Enterprise Finance Guarantee fund, for example, is expected to deliver £2 billion to SMEs by the time the scheme ends in 2014-15.[40] Like the ICFC, a future industry bank could act as a channel for greater SME investment and, after the initial cost of creation, it would fund its future through profits.

With the addition of state backing, though, it could also raise funds in the market cheaply, utilising rather than relying on this advantage to expand investment into as many SMEs as possible, in order to have the widest effect. Had the ICFC been offered state support, it could also have had an impact on the whole financial system and instituted a long-term change in the system's outlook. As it was, the ICFC coped well with the constraints imposed on it and managed to maintain an impressive record — something that should not be overlooked in the search for an improved model.

The regionalism of the ICFC should also be retained, as these were the key advantages that the Corporation had over commercial rivals. Currently, many commercial banks are accepting and rejecting loan applicants on the basis of the sector their production falls into. This is an oversimplified approach to investment and fails to appraise the merits of individual companies. A return to applicants being assessed by specialists would give SMEs a level playing field in terms of seeking investment and would benefit the banking sector as a whole. The Government should not be afraid of creating a new industry bank, nor of ensuring that its founding document prevents a loss of purpose.

The Macmillan Gap has not been closed since it was first identified 80 years ago and the problem is unlikely ever to be fully solved. Similarly, the short-termism of the British financial sector has failed to mature into one with a more long-term perspective. A new industry bank is required gradually to shift investment towards a more beneficial long-term perspective. As the ICFC showed, the indirect effects of its existence were as powerful as its direct investments, providing competition and therefore forcing the commercial banks to reassess their own approach to SME funding. The benefits of a new industrial bank should be seen in similar terms, providing an alternative model for others to follow as well as engaging with the SMEs. Again, for the true potential of an industry bank to be realised, government support would be necessary.

There is another issue to be considered—whether it is best to create one industry bank or multiple ones. The industry bank model is utility based: the bank would perform a necessary function that other commercial banks do not want. Without competition, a single industry bank would have no real incentive to strive for the best performance. Having multiple industry banks would ensure a competitive process that increased mutual learning. Indeed, this was the original hope of the Macmillan report which stated: 'There is no reason why the field should be limited to any one institution. In fact it is too wide for that to be desirable.'[41] This recommendation was never acted on. Multiple industry banks would have to be able to compete with each other to survive as well as, where possible, to compete with commercial banks.

2

The US Small Business Administration

Introduction

The United States has a very successful organisation dedicated to improving the lot of SMEs called the Small Business Administration (SBA). Unlike the now-defunct ICFC and the evolved KfW, the SBA is a national investment institution and official agency that has mostly retained its original form and aims continuously for the last 60 years.

Contrary to the image of America as the lair of feral capitalism 'red in tooth and claw' and mega-corporations, the US actually has a thriving SME sector. America officially defines any company with fewer than 500 employees as 'small'.[1] There are roughly 27.3 million small businesses in the US, employing over half of the American workforce, and representing 99.7 per cent of employer firms. About 43 per cent of all high-tech workers are found in SMEs and, in total, 97.5 per cent of exporters of goods are SMEs.[2]

The SBA was originally set up in 1953 as an independent agency by President Eisenhower, with the initial brief to: 'aid, counsel, assist and protect, insofar as is possible, the interests of small business concerns'.[3] It grew out of a previous institution, the Reconstruction Finance Corporation (RFC), which had been set up in 1932 by President Hoover to assist business affected by the Great Depression through federal lending programmes. The RFC was shut down just before the SBA's genesis, and the latter received a portion of the former's funds on its demise. Since then, the SBA has not deviated much from its original aim, and has supplied 20 million American SMEs with financial help. Additionally, it involves itself in providing small businesses with government contracts, although this will not be discussed in this report. At present, the SBA has roughly 219,000 loans worth around $45 billion, making it the largest investor in US businesses.[4] However, the SBA has not been universally appreciated. During the 1990s, under President Bush Snr, there was pressure to dismantle it, and while it survived, it was then starved of cash under President Bush Jnr. Since becoming President, Barack Obama has revitalised the Administration, raising its budget and enlarging its brief via the Small Business Jobs Act of 2010.

In light of the Act, the SBA has three updated goals:

(1) growing businesses and creating jobs;

(2) building an SBA that meets the needs of today's and tomorrow's small businesses;

(3) serving as the voice for small business.[5]

Like KfW, its aims are therefore explicit and its brief is clear.

The SBA divides the SMEs it wants to help into two main groups: the 'high-growth' and 'Main Street' categories. The reasoning behind helping the former is obvious—they have the potential to provide many future jobs and increase GDP. The latter group includes the shops and retailers located in central business areas.[6]

It is important to note that the SBA does not directly provide loans itself. Instead, it provides guarantees in case of default on loans made by the various lenders who have signed up to its guidelines. This means that those with bad credit histories are still unable to access finance, but the intention was never to overcome this, but rather to supply funds to creditworthy but otherwise neglected companies. For these successful borrowers, the SBA aims to make finance less burdensome, both by providing longer-term loans with correspondingly lower repayments and by requiring less collateral than standard commercial lenders.

While the benefits to the borrower are clear, the SBA's underwriting helps the commercial lender too, as they have their risk substantially mitigated. Given the indirect provision, the SBA has to keep the commercial banks onside, to keep them prepared to offer their guaranteed loans. This means the interest rate of SBA loans is above the commercial lending rate, to keep the banks interested, although the length of loan somewhat mitigates the borrower's pain. Given that by definition SBA-backed firms are unable to access this commercial finance anyway, the higher interest rate is somewhat moot. In light of the recession, the SBA has attempted to maintain banks' custom by also offering faster processing and improved customer service, to forge increasing bonds. This plan has worked and in 2010 it has attracted an extra 1,300 lenders who were either new or had not made an SBA loan since 2007.[7] By helping the banks, the idea is that the SBA helps SMEs.

Types of loan

The SBA offers two main types of loan to SMEs, the 7(a) and 504. A survey by the Urban Institute investigated how businesses spent the proceeds of SBA loans and found:

> The top uses for loan proceeds among respondents in the 7(a) programme were purchasing new equipment (34 per cent), financing working capital (23 per cent) and acquiring the original business (21 per cent). In the 504 programme, respondents most commonly built a new building (36 per cent) or purchased a new building (33 per cent); they also purchased new land (16 per cent) or new equipment (15 per cent).[8]

The 7(a) represents the bulk of SBA business and is provided when SMEs do not qualify for commercial loans and consequently struggle to raise finance. In particular, it is designed to meet the needs of start-ups and business owners facing special competitive opportunity gaps (such as female or ethnic minority owners, or those setting up in rural or distressed urban areas). These are the companies disproportionately ignored by commercial lenders. The 7(a) loans are made by the private sector and then backed by the SBA, which usually charges the borrower a fee for their services. This guarantee means that if the borrowing firm goes bust, the lender will receive a percentage of the investment back, normally from 50 to 85 per cent, effectively acting as collateral for the borrower. While the terms and conditions of the loan are set by the private lender, there are constraints imposed by the SBA, most notably on the variable interest rate, which is pegged to the prime lending rate (which in itself is pegged at three per cent on top of the federal funds rate). These are offered usually at higher interest rates than normal, commercial loans, but with significantly longer repayment terms. This programme provides loans of up to $5 million, with a maturity period of ten years for working capital and 25 years for real estate.

There are various special loan programmes that 7(a) covers, such as businesses in rural areas, but of most note is the Export Loan Programme which is provided through commercial lenders. SME exporters and any business that has been in operation for over 12 months can apply for export-specific loans of up to $500,000. Crucially, this does not mean they have to have been *exporting* for 12 months, and indeed the loan can be used to initiate their export ability, something that is normally quite an expensive process. These small loans could have a disproportionate effect on a company's business, providing the means to move from domestic to international manufacturer.[9] There is also the larger International Trade Loan, which is granted for growing exporters and 'small businesses that have been adversely affected by international trade and can demonstrate that the loan proceeds will improve their competitive position'.[10] Providing up to $5 million and guaranteed up to 90 per cent, this could provide once highly competitive SMEs with a lifeline to revitalise their business in the face of otherwise superior international competition.[11] Companies could use the money in myriad ways to regain the edge, such as by modernising their plants and equipment to bring down the cost of their goods and/or raise their quality.

The 504 loan programme is similar to the 7(a) programme, in that it too is designed for SMEs unable to obtain commercial finance, although it constitutes a smaller volume of loans: in 2010, for every dollar lent in the 504 programme, $2.6 were given out in 7(a) loans.[12] The 504 loan is expressly designed 'to encourage economic development within a community'.[13] It delivers this through long-term (10 to 20 years), fixed-rate loans allowing SMEs to grow via acquisition or modernisation of fixed assets. The loans are only available to invest in capital goods such as real estate or machinery but cannot be used to purchase working capital. Typically, borrowers apply for 504 lending to cover the cost of a pre-defined project. The money is then provided via one of 270 local non-profit organisations called Certified Development Companies, who work jointly with private lenders and the SBA to generate the funds.

The real advantage of the 504 programme is that the lender has to find only ten per cent of the project's costs, with the other 90 per cent being loaned through the SBA and private sector. The maximum amount available to borrowers depends on how the company fits in to public policy criteria and therefore how valuable it is to the national interest. For example, if the loan will enable the creation of jobs or increase competitiveness, the upper limit is $1.5 and $2 million respectively. $4 million is available to some firms who benefit the wider economy of the local area or can guarantee the creation/retention of one job per $400,000. These 504 loans are self-consciously about enriching the American economy as a whole, not just the firms involved. The SBA recognises that SMEs are part of a system that is worth more than the sum of its parts, and that for a strong national economy, strength must be created in all regions and sectors.

Small Business Investment Companies (SBICs)

In 1958, the Small Business Investment Act was passed by the US Government to establish the Small Business Investment Company (SBIC) programme, to be administered by the SBA. The original objective of this programme was very Cold War. It was to fill the gap between the needs of small business start-ups and the availability of venture capital, and by filling the gap and investing in small businesses, it was hoped that this would result in technological innovations to rival those from the Soviet Union.

In the present day, SBICs are privately owned and managed investment funds that are licensed and regulated by the SBA, using a combination of SBA-guaranteed funds and their own private capital funds to make equity investments in SMEs that qualify for such investment.[14] The investments can either be used to start new businesses or for the growth of existing ones, and the funds borrowed from the SBA are at very favourable rates.[15] The SBICs are profit-motivated businesses, hoping to share in the success of the small businesses in which they invest, and most are owned by small groups of local investors. Some are owned by commercial banks or corporations with publicly traded stock. The funds invested by the SBICs are in the form of debentures which are guaranteed by the SBA, and, importantly, these do not rely on taxpayers' dollars. The debentures are periodically pooled and sold to private investors on the public markets.[16] Taxpayers actually benefit from the activities of the SBICs, as the tax revenue created by the investments is greater than the cost of the programme, thereby benefitting the whole economy.

The involvement of the SBA in the SBICs is limited to their licensing and regulation—it has a minimal role in their day-to-day organisation. The SBA awards licences to SBICs on the basis of the capabilities and character of the applying management team and the availability of private capital. SBICs enjoy far greater flexibility in the financing options they can offer to small businesses: each investment is specifically tailored to the needs of the particular company.[17]

In October 2010, over 300 SBICs were licensed to provide long-term venture capital loans to small businesses, with a total capital of over $16 billion. The FY2010 volume of investments was the highest in the SBIC programme's history: a record $1.59 billion which was a 23 per cent increase on FY2009.[18] Between their establishment in 1958 and April 2009, SBICs had invested approximately $56 billion in over 100,000 small businesses. In comparison to the 7(a) and 504 loan programmes, however, the volume of investments from the SBICs is significantly lower.[19] Interestingly, SBIC investments have a much higher likelihood of being used in the manufacturing industry than the 7(a) and 504 loans, which are more likely to be used to finance technologies and innovations.[20] The percentage improvement in sales for businesses that have received SBIC funding, one year following investment, is substantially greater, at 54 per cent, than those that received 7(a) assistance, at just 18 per cent.[21] Furthermore, 74 per cent of those who received financing from an SBIC considered the loan to have been very important or somewhat important to the success of their business.[22] A 2008 study by Temkin and Theodos indicated that SBIC investments tend to be smaller, less concentrated in the technology sector, and less geographically concentrated than comparable investments made by private venture capital funds, and therefore the SBIC programme significantly contributes to the achievement of the SBA's aim to provide capital to businesses that are underserved by the private venture capital industry.[23]

The UK does have an existing analogy to the SBIC programme: the Enterprise Capital Funds (ECFs). These were set up in 2006 as a means of filling the equity gap via partnering government funds with private sector lending, up to a total of £2 million. ECFs are open to any firm that can demonstrate they suffer from the equity gap but are commercially viable businesses. However, there are certain sectors that are not permitted to seek ECF funding, which includes important industrial sectors such as steel and automotive manufacturers. In addition, if the company cannot find private sector backing within six months of the application, the government usually withdraws any offer for funding that exists, so the ECF is not a real model for increasing SME lending.

Role in combatting the recession

In 2012, the SBA has requested $985 million in funds from the federal government, a rise of 19 per cent on the 2010 budget. This increase was claimed as necessary due to the urgent need to invest in more businesses and revitalise the economy.[24] This new-found role as a cash-injector for SMEs was acknowledged in the Recovery Act of 2009 and Small Business Jobs Act of 2010. These saw the SBA's status significantly augmented in three main ways.

The fees payable by borrowers and some lenders for SBA loans were either reduced or even cancelled, with the cost being paid for by the government. This was noted by the SBA to be 'a popular programme', a somewhat unsurprising outcome.[25] Interestingly, the government money backing this reduction ran out repeatedly as businesses sought to take advantage of the offer, with the funding consequently topped up on multiple occasions.

Another important policy in generating demand was the increase of guarantee levels for 7(a) loans up to 90 per cent with a maximum backing of $1.5 million. The SBA reported that: 'this programme proved to be so effective in increasing lender interest in making small business loans that funding was extended multiple times'.[26] Both this and the reduced lending fees were extended for a *sixth* time in the Small Business Jobs Act. Given that the SBA relies on banks being willing to make these loans, this has been crucial to its resilience during the recession.

A new form of loan was also created in the Act entitled the 'America's Recovery Capital' (ARC) loan. This was designed to be a rapidly deployable loan of up to $35,000 interest-free that would be given to businesses to pay off other loans. Payback on the ARC is deferred for a year and then has a term of five years. The idea behind it was to ensure that previously successful firms who were beginning to miss (or were at risk of missing) monthly repayments would avoid defaulting. Because the loan is still paid out by commercial institutions, the SBA pays them interest throughout the term of the loan, effectively taking on the usual responsibility of the borrower. Eight thousand businesses benefitted from this in 2010 alone.[27]

What is most striking about the SBA during the recession is how the potential for an even worse crisis was averted. The whole mechanism of guaranteeing commercial loans could have ceased if the banks simply refused to lend and many SMEs would have gone without lifesaving funds as a result. It was thanks to the American government's repeated willingness to inject more funds into the SBA and promote its role that this situation was avoided.

Success and benefits

Without a doubt, the existence of the SBA had a positive effect on American SMEs, and the US economy is stronger for its continued role. However, the extent of this positive effect is not so easy to judge. In theory, it should be, if outcomes were measured, but the SBA itself has only ever focused on assessing output measures such as loans approved. This gives no indication of how beneficial the loans are and consequently if the SBA is meeting its primary objective of helping businesses grow. Using the basic measures available, such as who received loans, it would appear that the SBA is delivering to its target customers, i.e. those not receiving loans from commercial banks.[28]

Start-ups are a particularly good example of this as they lack collateral and consequently find commercial borrowing harder. This is due to the lack of information available to the bank about the companies involved. Without this information, the bank cannot assess the risk of the investment and therefore denies it outright. The longer the relationship with an existing small business, the more likely the bank is to grant them a loan or require less collateral, as information about the firm would have built up over time. The SBA has made a point of helping start-ups and its guarantees play an important part in this. From 2001-04, 25 per cent of 7(a) loans and 18 per cent of 504 loans were to start-ups compared to five per cent in the private sector.[29]

In addition, SBA loans are more accommodating of customers' needs, offering variable rates (for the 7(a) programme only) and filling the equity gap where most needed. For example, a third of 7(a) loans were between $50,001 and $150,000, while only a fifth of commercial loans were. Similarly, while almost 70 per cent of 504 loans were worth between $150,001 and $700,000, this made up only 20 per cent of commercial lending.[30] The two programmes are not designed to overlap, and this is successfully reflected in their loan sizes. The disparity between SBA and commercial lending is even clearer in maturity lengths, with almost half of all commercial loans maturing in a year or less, while the equivalent number of SBA 7(a) loans mature in five to seven years.[31]

Given the lack of official data, the SBA brought in a consultancy, the Urban Institute, to assess outcomes. It comprehensively analysed the effect of the loan on the average volume of firms' sales:

> The analysis found somewhat greater sales growth in years immediately following receipt of financing (e.g., the per cent change in sales between the year of financing and one year after financing was 18 per cent for firms in the 7(a) programme; it rose by 18 percentage points to 36 per cent by two years after financing, and then it only rose by six percentage points to 42 per cent by three years after financing.[32]

It would appear then that the SBA loans are having a beneficial effect on companies. Unsurprisingly, the short-term growth is rapid as the firms make use of the loan to increase their output. This levels off as the new rate of production is maintained rather than enlarged.

Pre-recession, the proportion of manufacturing companies receiving SBA loans was not much different to the proportion in the private sector: 8.3 and 8.9 per cent respectively from 2001-04. At that time, the market penetration of the SBA was also quite high. For every manufacturer receiving an SBA-backed loan, there were 1.6 firms that faced a capital opportunity gap.[33] This was significantly lower than in many other sectors such as financial services, which faced a ratio twice that size.

As a result of its organisation, the success of the SBA has in part relied on its cooperative stance with other commercial banks, as this delivered the majority of its business. A survey found that an average of 66 per cent of 7(a) and 504 borrowers heard about the existence of SBA funds via their bank.[34] Unlike the ICFC then, because the SBA does not tread on the toes of its commercial partners, it is provided with customers and the relationship is based on cooperation and mutual benefit. Importantly, these same customers did not believe that they would have been able to obtain the finance through commercial banks either, with an average of 44 per cent disagreeing with the statement that they could have found the loan elsewhere.[35] This would suggest that the SBA is fulfilling its aim of being the 'last resort' of SMEs and provides what the private sector will not.

Part of this remit also involves providing loans to businesses establishing themselves in 'underserved' areas. These are usually underutilised locations with populations on below-average incomes. Banks are usually wary of lending to businesses in such areas as the risks of failure are perceived as higher. Of course, from a state perspective, revitalising these regions is very important, and bringing in new businesses and consequential employment is a vital part of the regeneration process. It is of little wonder then that in 2006, 49 per cent of 7(a) loans went to such underserved areas, so again it would seem this goal is being achieved.[36]

Aside from the breadth of beneficiaries, the SBA's performance can be measured through the effect the loans have had. While the loans might not be the only factor involved, the results still speak for themselves:

> For 7(a), mean revenues rose from $1.3 million to $2.1 million; for 504, mean revenues rose from $2.7 million to $4.6 million. The median revenue in the 7(a) programme at the time of the loan was $300,000, rising to $500,000 currently, while the median for 504 respondents was $1 million initially, rising to $1.5 million currently. Mean full-time employees, for those reporting for both periods, rose

from 8 to 11 for the 7(a) programme, and from 16 to 22 for the 504 programme.[37]

The SBA was originally funded by government money, and the extent of this was measured in a subsidy rate. This is the number of taxpayer dollars needed to provide every $100 of loans and is calculated after the return on the investment is taken into account. The subsidy rate for 7(a) loans used to be around $5 in the early 1990s, but dropped off sharply to $0 from 2005, when it became a 'zero credit subsidy' programme, i.e. not requiring annual contributions from taxpayer funds.[38] After the financial crisis, despite the high levels of new funding provided to the SBA, the subsidy rate for the 7(a) programme rose only to 0.46 per cent in 2010 and remained at zero for the 504 loans.[39]

A voice for SMEs

The third aim of the SBA, to give a voice to SMEs, means the Administration is a two-way channel, not just giving governmental loans out, but listening to needs as well. This was formally implemented in 1976, when an Office of Advocacy was created within the SBA. This provides research and statistics into the small business activity in every US state and so has extensive knowledge about the state of the SME economy. The SBA is consulted on any major federal initiative likely to affect how SMEs do business and can consequently (in theory) mitigate negative issues. The cost of doing this is impressive. In 2010, for every million dollars saved by businesses, only $625 were spent by the Office.[40] In addition, this involves examining potential new regulations for SME-hindering red-tape, and informing the federal government of its findings.

When rules that jeopardise competitive ability are found, these too are tackled. For example, in September 2011, the Office of Advocacy expressed the concerns of some SMEs about new changes to the Proposed 'Occupational Injury and Illness Recording and Reporting Requirements of the Occupational Safety and Health Administration'. The proposed changes mean that 40,000 additional firms and 80,000 additional establishments (employing nearly 1.4 million additional employees) would be required to maintain a certain type of log of employee illness and injury, which would significantly increase the health and safety burden on small businesses.[41] Subsequent to meeting with representatives of small businesses to discuss the potential implications of the proposed changes, the Office of Advocacy sent a letter to the Occupational Safety and Health Administration to represent the businesses views. Such representation from an institution backed by the Federal Government is significantly more likely to have substantial impact on the proposals in comparison to a communication from one small business or even a large lobbying organisation. In total in 2010, the Office saved $14.9 billion in first-year costs and $5.5 billion in annually reoccurring savings.[42]

While the dissemination of industrial expertise to SBA clients does not occur to the same extent as it did in the ICFC, the SBA does have an indirect role here. The Service Core of Retired Executives (SCORE) is a voluntary organisation that provides businesses with knowledge and experience via mentoring. Founded in 1964, it currently operates with 360 chapters across the US and 13,000 volunteers.[43] SCORE operates on a non-commercial basis and does not charge clients for its services, offering a range from one-to-one business-mentor meetings to local workshops with regional experts, giving companies the benefit of all approaches. SCORE estimated that in 2010, its 600,000 business-owner clients created approximately 60,000 new firms, created 70,000 jobs and saved 20,000 more.[44] While this growth cannot of course be entirely attributed to SCORE, it is clear that it has had a positive impact and the SBA has attributed the creation of 1,100 new companies to SCORE in 2010 alone.[45] This is quite an achievement, especially considering the programme's relatively modest cost. In 2009, it had expenses of $10.4 million but raised $10.8 million, with federal grants making up only $5 million of this.[46]

Case study: Fiscal Year 2010

It is useful to examine the experiences of the SBA in the fiscal year of 2010 (FY2010), the latest year for which information is available and the first year that might be termed 'post-recession', where commercial lending and loan demand are still comparatively low. Using FY2010 also allows comparison with the equivalent experiences of Britain, and reveals the lessons to be learnt about industrial banks most clearly.

In total, the SBA reported that in FY2010: 'the Agency used $680 million of taxpayer funds to support $21.5 billion in approved loans supporting more than $30 billion in lending commitment to small businesses'.[47] In comparison with the previous year, this represents a dollar volume increase of 39 per cent and loan approval rates rising by 19 per cent. As discussed, this was mostly made possible by the Federal Government's new commitment to reenergising SME investment via the Small Business Jobs Act. Recovery funds formed the bulk of both forms of loans approved, with $10 million and $3.5 million in the 7(a) and 504 programmes respectively.[48]

This was roughly twice the amount anticipated, while the volume goal on non-recovery loans was failed significantly, by over half on both programmes. This weighting is perhaps unsurprising given the circumstances. Most revealing is the sole measure of success by outcome: the number of jobs supported through lending. In the 7(a) programme, 475,000 jobs were maintained, which was 24 per cent below target. On the 504 programme, the figure was 82,000 employees, 38 per cent below target.[49] Neither of these is an ideal outcome, and shows that while the volume of loans approved and firms helped was over target, the loans were not necessarily being used to the best effect.

Despite its somewhat lacklustre results, the SBA has been a success in helping to revitalise the US economy post-recession, and has gone some way towards satisfying demand, although it should be noted that demand for SBA loans fluctuates with time. Given that it only provides loans to those who, by default, cannot obtain them elsewhere, it has much more of a role in climates of recession, and less use when times are good. In 2006, for example, the SBA failed all its own lending approval targets, and this was the result of low demand for its products, rather than the fault of the agency.[50] However, given that many small firms in 2010 were retrenching rather than expanding, demand continued to be dampened. This is not necessarily a problem for such an explicitly backed institution, which has constant funds feeding into it, but would likely be avoided by an investment organisation able to attract and choose its own borrowers. On the whole though, the SBA has certainly provided a crutch to the economy.

Problems

The SBA is not able to make loans directly to its customers, and this is the Achilles' heel of the scheme. At the end of the day, the Administration is entirely reliant on the goodwill of the commercial banks to offer their loans, and if they decide not to take up the SBA's guaranteed backing, no matter how reasonable, then there is little the SBA can do. This issue has been seen in the 7(a) loan programme for lower sized loans up to the $350,000 mark. The SBA's 2010 Performance Report noted: 'smaller dollar SBA loans have fallen off in volume since 2007, in part because they are the costliest for lenders to make'. However, it also recognised that, '[these loans] also disproportionately benefit underserved markets, women-owned businesses and start-ups'.[51] This attitude from commercial lenders is unsurprising given 7(a) loans usually have comparatively high administration costs for low returns. The head of the SBA's Office of Capital Access once summarised: 'We're not trying to replace conventional lending, we're trying to make loans to creditworthy borrowers, not to lose money on the programmes.'[52] Because it does not compete, in the financial world, it is effectively servile and there is nothing within its current structure that can overcome this.

The need to appease the banks can be seen in SBA interest rates. Looking at loans of less than $1 million from 2001-04, the 7(a) interest rate was on average 1.8 percentage points higher than those of commercial loans. This was necessary to entice banks to make the loans to customers it would otherwise ignore, but it means the SMEs face a premium to obtain finance that could be seen as unfair but defended as a necessary evil. This means US companies are having to spend money on repayments that could be better invested in their own businesses.

Given that the SBA is unable to offer loans directly and has to work through middlemen, it is designed to be a 'last resort' for SMEs. While the work it does *is* very valuable, this passive stance is not the best approach, as it means the SBA is not in control of how potential customers are filtered through to it. This should not be a problem in theory: as the SBA relies on commercial banks first refusing to lend to borrowers, if a bank sets the lending criteria too high, then many more businesses will be forced to seek its aid. However, this was not the case in reality and the paralysis of the SBA could be seen as the recession fully hit in 2008. Crucially, banks preferred simply to refuse potential borrowers outright, and not refer them to the SBA, effectively denying them loans they could have received because it was not in their commercial interest. This meant the SBA's lending also fell significantly, from delivering 110,000 7(a) and 504 loans in FY2007 to just under 80,000 in 2008 and 48,000 in 2010.[53] As the principle method by which the federal government injected SMEs with cash, the weakness of the whole scheme was revealed.

This situation came about because the banks tightened their criteria for lending, while applicants' creditworthiness was also declining at the same time that the value of their collateral fell. This was the same reason for much of the wider fall in lending during the recession, and larger companies were similarly constrained. However, for SBA loans, in addition to the heightened risk, the rewards also decreased. As discussed above, the interest rate is fixed at an upper limit based on the prime lending rate, which was forced down by Federal Reserve cuts, so banks were not making as much on the loans. At the same time, this decimated the secondary market for SBA-backed loans as low interest rates combined with rising costs of raising capital to buy the loans. The outcome was therefore the same as if the SBA did not exist. Banks would no longer lend to firms even with long-standing relationships. Some evidence points to banks simply ignoring entire SME sectors, not bothering to distinguish between creditworthy and unworthy companies, or not having the information to do this.[54] This is a problem many UK SMEs regularly complain about as well.

The issue is an historical one. Traditionally, small companies were most often served by small, local banks that served regionally, not nationally, and knew clients well. They specialised in dealing with local businesses and so were tailored to understand and advise on this basis, much like regional branches of the ICFC. Due to the limited size of their assets, small loans were the bread and butter of these minor banks, so the relationship was valuable both ways. However, the number of these banks in the USA has been dwindling almost as long as the SBA has existed. In 1966, single-office banks, those most likely to limit investment to a single region, accounted for 10,000 out of roughly 13,000 banks. By 2008, this had fallen to 2,000 out of 7,200.[55] Since the recession, many of these two thousand have now gone bust: of the 250-odd banks failing from 2007-10, 150 had assets worth less than $500 million and there were 190 worth less than $1 billion, so small banks are even less prevalent.[56] This has been leaving SMEs reliant on the larger banks that have much less interest in providing them with loans, as big money can better be made elsewhere. So while the demand for SBA services has increased, the desire of banks to utilise them has not necessarily increased as well.

The only solution within the current system would be to raise the upper limit on the interest rate, which is a double-edged sword in itself. This would revitalise the appeal of the loans to banks on the basis of greater profits to be made, but would also increase the cost to borrowers who pay above average rates anyway. This duality, of satisfying the banks and borrowers, is a tension the SBA has not resolved and while some loans are now pegged to other rates, this has not fixed the underlying issue of how to help businesses without pandering to banks. Given the full value of 7(a) loans is not guaranteed though, there is still a fairly significant risk for the bank taking on the lending. In itself, this is reasonable to expect given that the bank still stands to make money out of the transaction. One solution could be to guarantee 100 per cent of the loan, but with no risk the loan takes on the image of a bond, making the bank unfairly easy profits. This would likely be unacceptable to the American public as it could be perceived as using taxpayers' money to subsidise financial institutions. More importantly, this would also undermine the need for due diligence on the bank's side, who could grant SBA loans to all comers, whether sound or not, as the government would pick up the tab for the failures. This is effectively the recipe for a sequel to the sub-prime lending crisis.

The 'last resort' nature of the SBA is not necessarily the best approach to financing SMEs for the national interest anyway. Pre-recession, *Business Week* reported that only one per cent of small businesses receiving finance did so through the SBA in a given year.[57] This otherwise rejected one per cent are not necessarily those with the most potential to contribute to the economy, and the SBA suffers from above-average default rates. From 2000-11, almost 12 per cent of all SBA loans were defaulted on, which is a number no ordinary commercial institution could stand, nor indeed could the ICFC or KfW.[58] While these less certain investments might benefit the nation in absolute terms, in relative terms there are far better companies to lend to if you want the maximum 'bang for your buck'. Of course, the SBA is not able to lend to these firms, who are monopolised by commercial lenders and never need SBA services. Unlike the ICFC then, the SBA cannot help the best performers by offering a lower interest rate or other preferential terms and so it cannot reach its own potential.

Similarly, while the SBA is designed to serve small firms of less than 500 employees, the bulk of its loans focus on micro-level companies. In 2006, 57 per cent of 7(a) loans went to firms with up to five employees, which is a rate 15 per cent higher than commercial lending. In a way, this is unsurprising, given that companies with one to four employees make up 61 per cent of all businesses in the US.[59] However, the SBA actually underserves all other forms of small business, from six to 499 employees, compared to commercial lenders by around five per cent.[60] The 504 programme slightly redresses this imbalance, providing 20 per cent of its loans to firms with five to nine staff; 25 per cent to those with 10 to 19 staff; and 20 per cent to those with 20 to 29 staff.[61] However, given 504 loans constitute a much smaller part of the SBA's business, while the overall SBA bias towards the smallest firms is good for these tiny companies, it is not necessarily beneficial to the wider economy. This is because these micro-businesses are not those most likely to use the loans to grow the enterprise and hire more employees: they are using the loans to entrench their position and stay alive. There is a fine balance in choosing whether to spend limited resources on preserving existing jobs or providing new ones, and it might be the case that the SBA has too conservative an approach.

Conclusion

In terms of a new national investment bank for Britain, the SBA has many lessons to teach us, with as many warnings as instructions. Regardless of its faults, the SBA is perceived as useful by American SMEs. Ninety per cent of 7(a) borrowers and 87 per cent of 504 borrowers felt that the loans were either 'very important' or 'important' to the success of their business when asked.[62] On this basis it has certainly helped the American economy to stay alive, although perhaps more as a life-support machine than an adrenaline shot. Nonetheless, when the recession hit, the SBA's track record meant there was a tried and tested means with which the federal government could pour money into the small businesses that make up the bulk of the economy.

The SBA is also something of a paradox. While what it does is good, it could be argued that it has the potential to be much more than just a last resort institution and therefore have a much wider impact on the American economy. However, such an active role was never proposed. While it does meet its general target of aiding small businesses, it only does this in a rather narrow sense, by acting as understudy to the wider lending market and dealing with the least commercially desirable customers with the least to offer the economy. Of course, this is not true for all SBA borrowers, and many high-growth start-ups have benefitted from its loans when all other lenders failed and have since gone on to employ and export; but these companies are not the mainstay of SBA business and the SBA cannot actively seek them out. This limits its usefulness.

The SBA claims its loans are designed to supplement rather than compete with commercial banks and while its current record is impressive, it could perhaps be increased by directly confronting the equity gap. Of course, there is no way to estimate how much more successful it would be in this, or what the political consequences of such an approach would be. However, based on the comparative experiences of the ICFC and KfW, it would appear that direct competition is a better approach. At best, the SBA can only second-guess the market and offer attractive packages to banks to ensure they continue to offer their loans. Rather than following the market, the SBA should be leading it.

3

KfW[*]

Introduction

The Kreditanstalt für Wiederaufbau (KfW), one of Germany's five biggest banks, should be considered an important model for the establishment of state-banks all over the world. KfW styles itself as a 'promotional bank' and in this context 'promotion' means the fostering of its customers. In 2010, KfW's balance sheet totalled over €400 billion, with €604 million cash reserves, and its promotional business in Germany and abroad amounted to €81.4 billion: a 27 per cent increase on the previous year.[1] Owned 80 per cent by the Federal Government and 20 per cent by the governments of the federal states, or Länder, KfW's loans and bonds are regarded as equivalent to commitments of the Federal Republic of Germany. Little wonder then that in 2011, and in several previous years, the bank was awarded the title of 'The World's Safest Bank' by Global Finance.[2] KfW is designed to put the promotion of the German economy above all else and this is illustrated by the extent of the support it provides: its domestic financing volume in 2010 totalled €64.3 billion, the largest volume in KfW's history. As KfW notes, the outcome has been significant: 'the demand generated by this financing resulted in maintaining an

---

[*] This chapter was written by Lucy Hatton, Researcher at Civitas

additional 1.0 million jobs in the entire German economy for one year'.[3] Responses from borrowers reflect this benefit and in 2010 a KfW survey revealed that 91 per cent of final commercial borrowers and 95 per cent of private customers reported overall satisfaction with the services provided by KfW.[4]

Because it is a state-owned institution, the government has a say in how KfW is run. It is governed by a five-member Managing Board, or Vorstand, which reports to a 37-member Board of Supervisory Directors, or Verwaltungsrat.[5] The Supervisory Board consists of government ministers (the positions of Chair and Deputy Chair are held alternately by the Federal Minister of Finance and the Federal Minister of Economics and Technology) and other officials, including representatives of the two houses of the German parliament, the Bundestag and the Bundesrat.[6] The governments of the Länder, which own 20 per cent of KfW, are represented by the members of the Bundesrat who sit on the Supervisory Board. The overtly political nature of the institution's management has implications for some of its operations, as discussed further below (see pp. 60-61).

The origins of KfW

KfW was established in 1948 by the American and British military governments during the occupation of West Germany following the Second World War. Its success and value as a state institution is demonstrated by the fact that it is the only remaining creation from the Bizonal period, when US and British occupation zones merged in 1947 jointly to tackle the problems of post-war reconstruction, with the banking system a paramount concern.[7] As part of this process, a compromise on how to deal with the issue was reached in 1948 in the form of a Reconstruction Loan Corporation called the Kreditanstalt für Wiederaufbau, which literally translates as 'Credit Institution for Reconstruction'.[8] This institution would be tasked with financing the regeneration of Germany using, in part, the funds of the European Recovery Programme (ERP), also known as the Marshall Plan. Inspiration for the KfW came directly from the Americans' own Reconstruction Finance Corporation, set up in 1932 to perform financing functions on behalf of the US government during the depression of the 1930s and the Second World War. As noted elsewhere in this report, this was the predecessor of the Small Business Administration.

The German authorities were tasked with setting up the KfW, and in October 1948 the KfW Law was passed by the German Economic Council. On 2 January 1949, the KfW took up its task and began providing sureties on loans in cases where ordinary credit institutions were unable or unwilling to provide the money, which was initially limited under the KfW Law to DM 1 billion, although this increased over subsequent years.[9] The initial finance was provided from Government and Relief in Occupied Areas (GARIOA) funds as the first counterpart funds were not available to be distributed until early 1950.[10] The counterpart funds were loaned out by the KfW and the repayment and interest from the loans were recycled back into the economy. Between the commencement of the KfW's operations and 31 December 1950, it received 3,200 credit applications and paid out DM 2.68 billion. In comparison with the operations of the ICFC in this period (623 loans amounting to £34 million or DM 408 million), the KfW appears significantly more successful, mostly because it was far less constrained.[11]

Post-war reconstruction

The first task of the KfW was to finance the reconstruction of Germany after the Second World War. It began by ploughing funds into the basic goods industries and general infrastructure: in the early 1950s, more than half of all of KfW's lending was to electricity producers, the coal mining sector and the steel industry.[12] Assisting these sectors contributed to the regeneration by providing the energy supplies other industries required to manufacture their goods, thereby benefitting the whole economy. By the end of 1951, KfW had provided DM 570 million for the coal industry at an interest rate of between 7 and 7.5 per cent, well below the market rate.[13] Without this input, the coal mining industry would have almost certainly been unable to obtain any finance for its reconstruction, and this would have meant no improvement in coal outputs and, consequently, a significant limitation to Germany's reconstruction efforts.[14] Half a billion DM were also lent to the agriculture and food sectors between 1949 and 1953. During this time, the standard and quantity of farming equipment increased substantially (the number of tractors increasing fourfold to 300,000), enabling the sectors to return to pre-war levels of productivity and for Germany to become more self-reliant in food.[15]

It is, however, important to point out that the KfW was rarely the sole financier of any reconstruction project, and would usually provide between 20 and 30 per cent of the required money whilst the rest had to be acquired through other means.[16] Nevertheless, it is clear that the loans granted by the KfW in its first few years were crucial to the 'economic miracle' of German post-war reconstruction. By 1954, its mission in this area was fulfilled, yet the German government was reluctant to dissolve the KfW as it was making such progress and had gained significant expertise in stimulating economic development.[17] The bank's brief, of increasing the nation's prosperity, was an open-ended target and so there was no reason to end this. Their wisdom meant the institution continued to provide a stimulus for the German economy.

However, there was one significant limit on KfW's reach. Like the SBA, the KfW could only provide assistance to those businesses unable to obtain loans elsewhere, to ensure that it was not perceived as a competitor to private banks. This was the reason why KfW was not explicitly given the title of 'bank'. Furthermore, the loans it provided had to be administered by the commercial banks so as to allow them to maintain their direct relationships with their clients, and to avoid the establishment of KfW alienating the banks.[18] In addition, the profits (although small) made by the banks through administering KfW's loans were able to be reissued as new loans, further boosting their economic advantages.[19] In essence, KfW was (in part) responsible for the economic reconstruction of West Germany by overseeing the distribution of US$1.4 billion of Marshall Aid[20] and maximising the benefits that could be reaped by providing such finance.

Modern KfW

Unsurprisingly, KfW today looks somewhat different to the institution created over 60 years ago by the occupying powers. Since 2003, the Kreditanstalt für Wiederaufbau is now KfW Bankengruppe, with several separate arms and objectives:

- The KfW Privatkundenbank, the largest of the KfW's business areas, covers promotional schemes for individuals and housing companies.

- The KfW Mittelstandsbank, the second largest, yet with the highest volume of lending, finances small and medium enterprises (SMEs) with a view to keeping the German economy strong.

- The KfW Kommunalbank finances municipal and social infrastructure to support structural change and public welfare.

- The KfW IPEX-Bank (an independent subsidiary) covers international business with export and project finance.

- The KfW Entwicklungsbank finances progress in developing and transition countries around the world.[21]

In 1986, KfW took a significant step in its institutional development by applying for an international credit rating, and was rated AAA, the highest rating possible, by the agencies Moody's and Standard and Poor's.[22] During the 1970s and 1980s, KfW saw its balance sheet total increase almost sevenfold from DM 25 billion in 1971 to DM 199 billion in 1989, and then further to €400 billion in 2010.[23] The current major funding source of its promotional business comes from its activities in the international capital markets.

SME promotion and the reconstruction of East Germany following German reunification

In the mid-1950s, KfW turned its attention to the promotion of SMEs, or the Mittelstand.[24] SMEs had long held an important position in the German economy and, as the basic goods industries were now, thanks to KfW's loans, able to raise their own finance, KfW could focus on improving the competitiveness and productivity of the SMEs.[25] SME promotion remains a fundamental feature of the work of KfW today through the work of the KfW Mittelstandsbank. In 2010, 99 per cent of German enterprises were SMEs. KfW considers them to be the 'backbone of the economy' and their sustainability to be decisive for continuous economic development: SMEs employ two thirds of the German working population.[26]

However, serious domestic promotion of SMEs could not be said to have commenced until the 1970s. At this point, two oil crises in Germany and a phase of high interest rates caused a shift in economic thinking and a realisation of the need to promote SMEs.[27] In response to pressures from the Federal Government and German parliament, in 1971 KfW launched its first credit programme specifically for the promotion of SMEs. The Mittelstand Programme, or M Programme, was refinanced exclusively using capital market funds, and enabled the extension of long-term investment loans to SMEs. The programme was designed to overcome the competitive disadvantages suffered by SMEs when it came to securing finance in comparison with large corporations.[28] When the M Programme was launched, its volume of commitments was DM 500 million, which had grown to DM 6 billion by 1989.[29] The rapid deployment of the M Programme was a direct result of political pressure and shows that, if used correctly, political will can act as a very effective instrument for guiding KfW and, by association, the German economy.

From 1990, a key priority of KfW was the reconstruction of East Germany, or Aufbau Ost, the biggest modernisation programme in Germany's history, which centred specifically around SMEs.[30] Although the entirety of Germany had received Marshall Aid, the Soviet Union had banned the states of the Eastern Bloc from making use of any funds. Therefore, whilst the benefits of the counterpart funds were being felt all over West Germany, the Eastern states were somewhat left behind. Fortunately, the repayments of the long-term investments made by KfW following the War were continually reinvested, meaning that following German reunification in 1990 there was substantial finance available for reconstruction projects, particularly with regard to SMEs. East Germany had, at the time the Berlin Wall fell in 1989, virtually no SMEs due to several waves of expropriation. Consequently, per capita earnings in East Germany in 1990 were less than half of those in West Germany. An SME sector had to be established from scratch in East Germany to ensure the successful consolidation of the East and West German economies, a task taken on with zeal by KfW. Between 1989 and 1997, KfW provided finance to support 65,000 SMEs based in East Germany and over DM 50 billion in loans was granted to eastern SMEs, creating or securing 2.5 million jobs in the new German states.[31] By 1990, approximately 70 per cent of KfW's domestic promotional funds were being put to use in East Germany.[32] Through its financing, KfW significantly contributed to the establishment of a thriving SME sector in East Germany.

Unconfined to just SMEs, KfW also provided for the modernisation of East German infrastructure with low interest loans, as mandated by the German Federal Government. The legacy of this programme means that East German municipal infrastructure today is more modern than that of West Germany and it continues to develop apace. In total, through its SME promotion, financing of infrastructure and contribution to the improvement of the housing sector, KfW has provided loans amounting to over €161.5 billion for the eastern states, significantly contributing to the reconstruction of East Germany and the swift success of German reunification.[33]

Other services: providing housing and helping the environment

Alongside its industrial programme, KfW juggled more socially targeted lending, showing that one state-owned institution can focus on multiple priorities. Throughout its history, KfW has used its funds to pursue housing reconstruction. In 1950, one out of every ten homes in West Germany benefitted from funds provided by KfW for development and modernisation, and 350,000 houses were constructed using KfW financing. One hundred thousand loans for housing projects were granted in 1990 alone, making KfW's programme of housing regeneration and modernisation the largest in the world.[34] By 2003, over 3.6 million homes in East Germany had benefitted from KfW funds, equal to more than half of all houses standing in the East when the Berlin Wall fell.[35]

KfW's programmes of housing modernisation and construction are inextricably linked with its emphasis on environmental protection. The housing modernisation projects financed by KfW in the 1990s always contained aspects of energy-saving insulation and modern heating technologies which had little adverse effect on the environment compared to what had existed before.[36] The 'Housing, Environment, Growth' Initiative of the Federal Government was launched by KfW in 2006 to further this process by reducing CO_2 emissions through energy-saving modernisation measures for housing.[37]

Protecting the environment has thus also been a longstanding objective of KfW. In the early stages of postwar reconstruction, KfW provided substantial loans to the agricultural sector, in order to improve rural infrastructure and ensure continued food supplies following the scarcity of the Second World War.[38] Its financing of agricultural projects to improve sewage disposal and water purification served environmental protection objectives, and by the end of 1960 KfW had invested half a billion DM in such environmental projects.[39]

Not only was KfW the first German bank to promote the environment, it has gone on to be the largest and most successful. It aims to fund projects that benefit environmental and economic development equally, and as such KfW will not promote any projects that are likely to cause environmental damage.[40] Around one third of KfW's total financing volume is invested in environmental and climate protection, in Germany and abroad.[41] In 2010, this amounted to €25.3 billion, including loans of €1.2 billion granted for specific investments in environmental and climate protection.[42] All KfW bonds are known as 'green bonds', which is considered a reassurance to environmentally concerned investors.[43]

Since 1996, however, KfW's housing focus has shifted away from construction and modernisation and towards ownership. The KfW Home Ownership Programme provides inexpensive funding to supplement loans provided through the borrowers' own banks by up to 30 per cent.[44] Between the start of the programme and 2010, more than one million home purchasers have benefited from the programme, predominantly young families unable to purchase their own homes through other means.[45] The success of KfW in helping people to get onto the property ladder has contributed to Germany's avoidance of the property market bubbles that have been seen in the UK over the last decade.[46]

The beginning of the 2008 financial crisis

A major embarrassment for KfW came in 2008 at the beginning of the financial crisis. On 15 September, KfW made an automated payment of €319 million (£248 million) to US bank Lehman Bros, just 14 minutes after it had filed the biggest bankruptcy case in US history.[47] The transfer was part of a standard currency swap arrangement, in which Lehman Bros was supposed to transfer $500 million to KfW in return, yet, due to its insolvency, the money never arrived. This resulted in a net loss of €536 million for KfW.[48] These losses followed KfW's controversial decision to sell IKB Deutsche Industriebank AG in August 2008 to Lone Star Funds for less than 20 per cent of the price the Federal Government had initially sought. KfW's earlier attempted rescue of the bank had caused a financial loss of €6 billion in 2007: the first financial loss in KfW's history.[49] A further financial loss of €2.7 billion occurred in 2008, in part due to the Lehman Bros transfer, among other unfavourable circumstances.[50]

KfW was nicknamed the 'world's dumbest bank' in response to the debacle, but it argued that the automated nature of the payment meant that it would have been very difficult to prevent, and that the insolvency of Lehman Bros came as a complete surprise.[51] Nevertheless, on 18 September the Federal Government requested the resignation of two members of the KfW Managing Board, Peter Fleischer and Detlef Leinberger, along with the head of Risk Management, who had failed accurately to calculate the risk of the Lehman Bros' insolvency.[52] In October 2008, an investigation was launched and the KfW headquarters were raided, whilst KfW's CEO hired legal representatives to probe the possibility of criminal charges being brought against Fleischer and Leinberger for their failure to prevent the transfer.[53] However, the investigations were concluded approximately two years later as the prosecutors declared that there was insufficient evidence of any intentional wrongdoing on the part of KfW.

Nonetheless, the transfer and its losses were highly embarrassing for KfW and consequently also for the German Federal Government, as a transfer of that size would probably have needed to be approved by the top bosses, which in KfW's case implicates several government ministers. Questions have subsequently been raised about the implications of the heavy involvement of the government in the management of such an institution, when it can lead to embarrassment on the scale of KfW's transfer to Lehman Bros. Still, the continued unequivocal support of KfW by the Federal Government meant that, despite the consequent financial losses, KfW retained its safe reputation and they did not impact upon its creditworthiness.

Even though the Federal Government explicitly uses KfW in the pursuit of its economic policy goals (as in the delivery of the government's economic stimulus packages during the financial crisis), historical examples exist which suggest that the involvement of the Federal Government in KfW has been overbearing, and at times KfW has resisted government instruction and threatened to withhold its services.[54] This implies that the relationship between the Federal Government and KfW has not always been perfectly harmonious, and whilst the government can be embarrassed by the actions of KfW, KfW can resist the instruction of the government.

Beyond the financial crisis

SME promotion in recent years has continued to boom. In 2010, KfW financed a record €28.5 billion for SMEs, amounting to approximately 94 per cent of all of KfW's commitments for the year.[55] This helped to continue the economic revival following the financial crisis of 2008-9 and led to the creation of 66,000 new jobs in the SME sector, adding to the 1.3 million jobs that the funds already helped to maintain. The resilience of German SMEs through the crisis could be said to be partly due to the assistance of KfW with long-term investment loans granted on incredibly favourable terms with working capital finance.[56] The distribution of the loans illustrates that those sectors hardest hit by the crisis received the greatest proportion of the assistance, for example metal production and processing received 13 per cent of the total, and automotive and mechanical engineering 12 per cent.[57] KfW played a pivotal role in the delivery of the Federal Government's economic stimulus packages designed to combat the financial crisis, the largest in Germany's history. The Federal Government authorised KfW to provide loans up to the volume of €52.5 billion in 2009-10 in the context of the stimulus packages.[58]

One of the provisions currently offered for SMEs by KfW is the KfW Start Up Loan, or StartGeld Programme, through which KfW assumes 80 per cent of the credit risk from the entrepreneurs' personal banks. The StartGeld Programme is designed to mitigate the disadvantages entrepreneurs face in obtaining finance to start up their businesses. It is not always in the interest of banks to award the small loans required by the majority of start-up businesses, and they are considered high risk due to the lack of collateral. In 2010, the amount financed under the programme totalled €220 million, distributed between approximately 7,100 start-ups.[59] By definition, examples of the programme's success are rather mundane. In 2010, one such would be the lending of €20,000 to a young hairdresser to enable her to start her own hair salon, which has since been very prosperous.[60] Without the assistance of KfW, it is doubtful that such enterprises like this hair salon would have been able to commence business so soon following the financial crisis. KfW StartGeld loans are, as with the reconstruction investments in the post-war period, applied for and paid out through the applicant's personal bank, so KfW is not directly competitive in this area. It is also down to the bank's discretion whether or not the loan is granted, based on the quality of the investment and the provided collateral.[61] In 2010, 436,000 new businesses started up in Germany, an increase of 66,000 (eight per cent) on 2009, resulting in the creation of 582,000 full-time jobs. Of the one-fifth of these start-ups that required external financing, 25 per cent received assistance from KfW or one of the regional promotional banks, inevitably contributing to German job creation.[62]

Similarly, the ERP Start Fund helps young companies with no collateral to obtain financing to develop new technologies. Through this programme KfW provides financing of up to €6 million for the technological development as a co-investor (of up to 70 per cent), on the same terms as that of the other investor.[63] In 2010, the ERP Start Fund financing volume totalled €80 million, an increase of €9 million on the previous year.[64] The programme therefore allows businesses to make progress in their industries when they would otherwise be unable to do so. In contrast to the KfW StartGeld Programme, financing from the ERP Start Fund is applied for directly through KfW and not the applicant's own bank.[65] In 2010, direct loans from KfW to customers, including those as part of the ERP Start Fund, totalled almost €101 billion, and indirect loans on-lent through commercial banks over €150 billion.[66] Whether or not the loan is administered directly or indirectly is dependent on the type of loan, as different loan programmes have different application and administration procedures.

A key contribution of KfW to economic recovery following the financial crisis came from the KfW Special Programme. The Special Programme was launched at the end of 2008 in the context of the Federal Government's economic stimulus packages, 'Securing Jobs by Reinforcing Growth', or Beschäftigungssicherung durch Wachstumsstärkung, which aimed to improve the availability of loans for companies in an attempt to compensate for the insufficient lending activity of commercial banks due to the financial crisis. The assistance was provided in the form of subsidised public loans of up to €50 million per project (although more can be provided in exceptional circumstances), and up to 100 per cent of the expected expenditure of the recipient. As with the funds from the StartGeld Programme, loans provided through the Special Programme were applied for and administered through commercial banks. The early stages of the Programme exceeded expectations fivefold and it was extended in March 2009.[67] By the end of 2010, almost 5,000 applications amounting to €13.3 billion had been approved through the Special Programme, of which almost €6.2 billion was from 2010 alone. The vast majority (94 per cent in 2010) of the loans went to support SMEs, and the investments had a significant impact on employment as they secured approximately 1.2 million jobs.[68] For this reason KfW considers that the Special Programme was a significant contributor to the prevention of a national credit crunch and the swift recovery of the German economy following the financial crisis.[69] However, as the German economic recovery had continued throughout 2009 and 2010, the KfW Special Programme, having fulfilled and even exceeded its targets, was closed at the end of 2010.

An additional provision of KfW is advice through the scheme Beratung in Krisen, or Counselling in Crisis. Struggling SMEs are able to approach KfW for the advice of an external management consultant when unforeseen economic difficulties arise. KfW provides a grant of up to €1,600 to cover the fees of the consultant, who attempts to identify the weaknesses in the company, the reasons for the difficulties and mechanisms for overcoming them.[70] Enabling SMEs in crisis to access vital business advice is a significant contribution on the part of KfW to the continuing success of the German SME sector.

Financing exports

Export financing began in 1950 in an attempt to enable German exporters to compete once again on the international markets. Following a brief diversion of export financing activities, KfW resumed activity in this area in 1953. Commercial banks were only willing to provide short-term financing commitments to German exporters, so KfW aimed to finance export transactions on a medium or long-term basis, as the promotion of exports was considered to be in the interest of the national economy. In the mid- to late 1950s, KfW's export financing activities expanded rapidly, and by the mid-1960s the total annual volume of export financing commitments had risen to over DM 1 billion, from DM 106 million a decade earlier.[71] This is arguably in part due to KfW's switching from providing supplier credits, that is, loans to the German exporter, to buyer credits: loans to the foreign importer. Through the 1970s and 1980s, the export financing commitments of KfW increased more than fivefold, no doubt evidencing the achievement of the objective of reviving German export industries.

Almost half of German economic output today is dependent on exports, and one in four jobs is dependent upon the success of German products abroad.[72] As such, KfW's export financing activities have in recent years developed through the activities of the legally independent subsidiary, KfW IPEX-Bank. In 2010, the volume of lending in the area of export and project financing totalled €59.8 billion, slightly less than that of 2009 (€63.6 billion).[73] The ERP Export Financing Programme, which is still financed today using reinvested money from the Marshall Funds, is used specifically to finance exports to developing countries in order to support both German exporters by enabling them access to new markets, but also the development and industrialisation efforts of the importer country.[74] For example, in 2010, over €10 million was provided to the Republic of Ghana for their purchase of over 150 vehicles that have been converted into ambulances by the German company Wietmarscher Ambulanz- und Sonderfahrzeug GmbH.[75] Federal export guarantees are provided by export credit insurance agency Euler Hermes as a means to mitigate the risks of the importer defaulting. Hermes Cover does not have a minimum order volume, so SMEs are not discriminated against in that way.[76] KfW also provides other financing opportunities for small exporters in order to further assist the development of SMEs. Since 2009, small export finance has been available in the form of buyer loans from between €0.5 million to €5 million over two to five years in cooperation with Northstar Europe, which provides fast track buyer credit cover for the SMEs.[77] Financing the exports of SMEs has further contributed to their continued success and development and their apparent resistance to the financial crisis.

Conclusion

KfW has certainly played a significant role in ensuring the continued success of the German economy throughout its history: from the post-war reconstruction of West Germany, through the restructuring of East Germany following reunification, to mitigating the difficulties of the 2008 global financial crisis. The assistance provided by KfW has been particularly beneficial for SMEs, housing and environmental protection within Germany. Its foray into international development and aid has also, it seems, been very successful. Based on its history, evident success and the extent of its financing capabilities, it is not difficult to see why KfW is considered to be a model example for the establishment of promotional industry banks in other countries around the world.

Many lessons can be learnt from the successes and struggles of KfW in relation to the possibility of a new national investment bank in the UK. For a start, KfW has successfully adapted its role and priorities over time effectively to serve the German economy in whatever way is required at that point in time. KfW is as supportive of the German economy as it was when it was first established over 60 years ago, if not more so. A British investment bank would do well to learn from this and be prepared to adapt its assistance for British industry to overcome not just the present challenges, but any that arise in the future. Only in this way can the longevity of the institution be ensured as well as the continued growth and success of SMEs.

Furthermore, KfW serves as a successful example of the effective balancing of environmental and economic priorities. It demonstrates that the pursuit of climate and environmental protection need not be abandoned in order to promote the German economy, but through expecting a certain level of green commitment in the projects it finances, KfW serves the dual purpose of supporting the economy and the environment. A similar British institution should take heed of KfW's example here and accept that more than one priority can be pursued simultaneously and to great effect. A national investment bank in the UK could easily support the reduction in carbon emissions and the growth of British industry.

Nevertheless, the case of KfW also contains warnings for a future British investment bank. KfW's close ties with the German Federal Government may be beneficial in the pursuit of the government's economic policies, as KfW's role in the delivery of the economic stimulus packages following the financial crisis demonstrates. However, the relationship can also lead to embarrassment and the possibility of the institution's reputation being protected by the government when this is not necessarily in the public's interest, as may have been the case during the investigation of the controversial Lehman Bros transfer. Any government establishing a British investment bank of a similar nature would need to think carefully about what the precise relationship between itself and the institution should be, bearing in mind the lessons that can be learned from the case of KfW.

Part Two
The Model of the Enterprise Bank

4

Existing British Institutions Aimed at Alleviating the Macmillan Gap

The Green Investment Bank: a separate model

Presently, the Government is intending to create a Green Investment Bank (GIB), which will be a mechanism to fund the growth of the low-carbon economy via investment in key areas. It will be set up effectively as an industry bank, but with a narrow remit. While its work will be similar to that of the Enterprise Bank (EB), it is an institution that deserves to stay separate.

The original outline, as announced in the June 2010 report *Unlocking Investment*, stated that the GIB's central aim is to 'support the delivery of the UK's emission reduction targets as set by the Climate Change Act 2008'.[1] In other words, the GIB is to help Britain meet the target of reducing emissions on 1990 levels by 34 per cent by 2020 and 80 per cent by 2050. In investment terms, the GIB's founding aim was 'identifying and addressing market failures limiting private investment in carbon reduction activities'.[2] This very vague goal was narrowed in the later *Update on the design of the Green Investment Bank* to mean:

- Risk mitigation products to present more attractive risk profiles to a wider range of investors.
- Innovative mechanisms to overcome high transaction costs of investment and share risks.

- Capital provision via either equity or debt, where shortages of capital remain.[3]

The National Loan Guarantee Scheme: an insufficient model

The 2011 Autumn Statement by George Osborne, Chancellor of the Exchequer, saw the announcement of the National Loan Guarantee Scheme (NLGS). This is aimed at lowering the cost of bank loans for businesses with a turnover of less than £50 million. This is possible through allowing banks to raise capital for loans on the wholesale money market using the Government's AAA credit rating, with the Government guaranteeing the funds and taking on the risk. As with KfW, piggy-backing on the back on this sterling rate means that finance can be raised at the lowest cost, and the intention is that this saving is passed on to the borrower. Unlike KfW though, the advantage of this lower cost is not being maximised. The Treasury has estimated that 'this will lead to a reduction of up to one percentage point on the cost of the business loan'.[4] In total, up to £20 billon of funding will be raised this way, over a two-year period with the possibility of an extension up to £40 billion.

The problem is that this does not even try to alleviate the funding gap. Rather than focusing on encouraging banks to lend, the NLGS insists that loans be made cheaper, meaning little change in return for the bank. If the bank is not able to make much extra profit out of the loan (however unsavoury this might appear to the borrower) then there is no extra motivation for the bank to actually provide these loans. The scheme almost appears to play to the perennial excuse of the commercial banks that there is not enough demand for loans, and that by lowering the interest rate, this demand will be created. The Government should realise that the lending crisis is a supply-side problem, not a demand-side one. Secondly, the guarantee here is to those supplying money to the banks, not the banks themselves. This means that if the bank fails, the creditor will receive their money back from the UK Treasury, but if the SME receiving the loan fails, the bank still has to face the loss. Overall, the NLGS therefore fails to mitigate the risk of lending to SMEs and cannot be relied upon as a means to close the Macmillan Gap. Instead, all it is likely to do is make borrowing easier for those already likely to receive loans; it will not increase the volume of loans granted. It would be far better for SME lending if the NLGS is never initiated, and the money, time and effort is rerouted to creating the Enterprise Bank.

Other new institutions that should be subsumed in the EB

While the GIB could be left alone, there are other schemes that should be ended, with their responsibilities and funding transferred to the EB. The Enterprise Finance Guarantee is the most important example of this, as a recent innovation that is beginning to have an impact on the British economy. While far longer established, the Export Credit Guarantee Scheme should also be subsumed. Maintaining individual institutions is highly inefficient and wasteful, given that the EB would be able to provide all the functions outlined below. It is also unproductive on the business side, as companies are forced to shop around to cater for their various needs, losing time and money better spent on maintaining production. This would simplify the whole spectrum of state investment mechanisms into one organisation and hopefully remove a great deal of the bureaucracy that surrounds access to these at present.

The Enterprise Finance Guarantee (EFG) scheme is a typical example of an existing scheme that would work more efficiently as part of the EB. It was launched by the Labour Government in November 2008 to replace the previous Small Firms Loan Guarantee (SFLG) scheme. The EFG Scheme is an attempt to facilitate bank lending to SMEs which lack the security required for a normal commercial bank loan. The scheme began on 14 January 2009 to help the SMEs through the tightened credit conditions at that time and to encourage their growth and prosperity as the economy recovers. The statutory basis for the EFG scheme comes from the Industrial Development Act of 1982. Individuals are not eligible for EFG loans; they are available only for SMEs.

Under the scheme, the government will guarantee 75 per cent of a loan of between £1,000 and £1 million, over three months to ten years, for a viable business with an annual turnover of less than £25 million. The business must be unable to provide any or sufficient securities to the lender to receive a standard commercial bank loan, but the bank must be satisfied that it would have provided conventional finance but for the lack of securities. The bank must guarantee the final 25 per cent of the loan. Thus the use of the EFG facilitates funding that would not otherwise take place. The EFG can be for new loans, the refinancing of existing loans, conversions of overdrafts, or the guarantee of invoices or overdrafts. The decision on whether or not to grant the loan and whether to use the EFG is down to the lender. There is an approved list of participating lenders that can be approached for financing under the scheme. The borrower must pay a two per cent annual premium on the outstanding loan balance, on a quarterly basis and in advance, to cover some of the costs of providing the guarantee. There are no pre-determined interest rates, they fall to the discretion of the lender. The EFG should be seen as protection for the lender in the event of the borrower defaulting; it should not be considered insurance for the borrower in the event of being unable to repay the loan.

The EFG was initially going to run until 2010, but has been extended by the Coalition Government and is currently in place until 2014-15. In 2011-12, £600 million is expected to be lent to around 6,000 recipients. Between the beginning of the scheme and 31 March 2010, £1.3 billion was available to be guaranteed. A further £700 million was available between 1 April 2010 and 31 March 2011, followed by the £600 million for 2011-12. Fifteen thousand loans totalling over £1.5 billion were offered through the scheme between its inception and June 2011, with the average loan offered £100,900. Not all of these loans were actually drawn: 13,720 loans were drawn totalling 'just' £1.3 billion. The majority of loans, more than 70 per cent, are for sums of less than £100,000. All sectors can be said to have benefited from loans under the scheme, for example, 18.7 per cent of the value of the loans drawn are for the manufacturing and production sectors.[5]

However, year on year, a drop in demand for loans under the EFG scheme of 40 per cent has been recorded, with a drop of 48 per cent in the volume of financing provided. The average size of the loan drawn also dropped by seven per cent: in the second quarter of 2010, the average loan size was £99,700, whereas in the second quarter of 2011, this had fallen to £93,200.[6] If the figures continue at this level, the EFG scheme will struggle to provide finance amounting to more than half of the £600 million for 6,000 recipients expected to receive loans in the 2011-12 financial year. The reasons for the decreases are unclear; however they do indicate that the EFG scheme may not be as successful in supporting SMEs as the Government has hoped.

The Coalition Government has extended the EFG scheme to create a new scheme, the Export Enterprise Finance Guarantee (ExEFG) Scheme, launched on 28 April 2011 to facilitate the provision of export financing to viable SMEs that lack the securities that would usually be necessary for such financing on an entirely commercial basis.[7] Accredited lenders can provide export finance loans from between £25,000 and £1 million for a term of up to two years. The Government guarantees 60 per cent of these loans under the ExEFG scheme, and the borrower must pay an upfront premium of three per cent per annum in exchange for the guarantee. In contrast to the EFG Scheme, the ExEFG Scheme operates as a commercial scheme on a non-aid basis so it is not restricted by EU state aid rules, and loans are therefore available to all business sectors.

5

What Should the Enterprise Bank Do?

Britain still retains many successful SME manufacturers. If we take 'small' companies to mean less than 50 employees, these account for 93 per cent of all British manufacturing firms, while non-SMEs only employ 1.2 per cent of the manufacturing workforce (or 0.06 per cent of the total UK workforce).[1] This is highly significant. Given that the larger the company, the easier it is to access capital of some form or another, this means that the vast majority of manufacturers are likely at some point to face the challenge of raising funds from otherwise unwilling banks. Many find this virtually impossible, and growth has to be funded through saving profits, which frequently takes a long time. Alternatively, firms can simply continue to produce goods at maximum capacity and turn down extra orders. For companies with proven abilities, both of these situations are very frustrating. It is foolish for the UK not to provide the means to improve its own economy, and even more so when one considers that the solution is so easily within our reach via the EB.

It is not the intention of this report to go into the minutiae of how the EB should be run and funded or what it should offer. These points are for discussion once the general shape of the EB has been fleshed out. Regarding its funding mechanisms, it will be assumed that 'loans' and 'equity finance' are the two key financial tools the EB will use. Because the bank will be lending on a 'case-by-case' basis, it would make sense to offer unique interest rates to different borrowers rather than posit general rates. While some very strong firms might merit low rates, other high-risk ones might require above average ones.

There are three main roles that the EB should take on in its role as economic catalyst. This trinity of funding, mitigating risk and providing advice are all intimately linked. Without any one of them, the bank would not meet its potential.

Fill the equity 'gap'

The equity 'gap' was the *raison d'être* for the ICFC being set up, and remains a key reason for the EB's creation. The financial experience of the last seventy years shows that nothing has changed and commercial banks are no more willing to enter that market. Clearly, something else has to fill the gap again, and this time, permanently. The EU itself has acknowledged an equity gap of some form exists post-recession, and therefore altered its state-aid rules accordingly, opening the way to the EB.[2]

In the present day, the goal posts have shifted with inflation. The gap now appears between £250,000-500,000 and £2-3 million. It is possible to raise hundreds of thousands of pounds from friends, family, re-mortgaging and other sources but after this, institutional investors only enter the picture when millions of pounds are being asked for: anything less than this is too small for them to bother with as the returns do not warrant it. The EB's involvement in the equity gap is likely to be its most significant role given that such projects would likely be completely or nearly all funded by the EB.

WHAT SHOULD THE ENTERPRISE BANK DO?

The equity gap is in part caused by 'credit rationing', where banks refuse to lend to creditworthy firms. This is often caused by an information deficit: banks do not examine a business's finances thoroughly enough and write them off, regardless of their ability. This is most likely to occur with small businesses, about which information is hard to come by without a site visit. Unsurprisingly, many banks are unwilling to invest the time and money which could eclipse the financial returns of investing. As a result, applicants are often rejected without a full hearing, no matter how high an interest rate the borrower would be willing to pay.

It is very hard to pin down the exact prevalence of this credit rationing, although it is clearly widespread. The American Government Accountability Office summarised the US problem: 'Studies we identified that empirically looked for evidence of credit rationing within the conventional US lending market, almost all provided some evidence consistent with credit rationing.'[3] However, it concluded that the studies had too wide-ranging definitions of what 'credit rationing' actually meant. Some described it as all rejected applications from SMEs while others critiqued this approach, as any number of other, valid reasons could lead to rejection. For the EB, all that matters is that credit rationing and the wider equity gap exist and must be overcome, as they were by the ICFC. The exact size of the gap is fairly irrelevant. Visiting small companies is not profitable, but the EB is aimed at maximising impact on businesses, not profit. Getting to know a company's ability before investment is vital to knowing the level of risk and therefore pricing interest on the loan correctly. Over-charging businesses for the EB's services should be avoided at all costs. In addition, visitations are the first step down the path towards being able to provide knowledgeable advice, so are really the cornerstone and 'USP' of the EB.

Risk

Another significant barrier for many firms attempting to secure investments is the perceived risk involved. High-growth firms are also often high-risk. If the EB's lending ethos is constructed along the same lines as the ICFC, i.e. decisions are based on industrial experts' opinions, this could mitigate the problem. If a company could secure an investment from the EB, this would be a symbol of faith in its future success from those most in the know.

This would have a benefit for the company beyond the money itself: if the EB investment is made public, then a shrewd investor could cash in on the opportunity, by offering further funds on more favourable terms than they otherwise would. These would allow companies to augment loans or find more equity for less loss of control. By providing this intangible public service, the EB could see its assets going further. For instance, knowing that a company could secure further funding after providing the initial outlay, it could offer around 50 per cent rather than 100 per cent of the required sum. The saved money would then allow another firm's needs also to be met.

Advice

Critics of the 'equity gap', who claim no such thing exists, often claim that the problem is not the lenders but the borrowers, and there is a kernel of truth to this. They argue that investors have the money to invest, but it is the good projects to invest in that are hard to find. The majority of would-be borrowers attempt to secure finance prematurely or without thinking their business plan through, which ends in their rejection. Some companies might genuinely hit a natural barrier where further development will not reap rewards, but the majority will fail for less structural reasons such as overestimating their potential.

These barriers can be overcome if the company is steered in the right direction. While by no means the mainstay of the EB's work, there is a lot to be said for the bank using its knowledge to help the most promising incubations who apply too early for funding actually to reach the position from which their application would be successful. This cooperative approach is much more desirable than an outright 'you're not ready yet' rejection. The benefits for the bank are obvious. By providing their expert advice, (payable perhaps through a marginally higher interest rate on eventual loans) the risk of the venture is reduced.

A failing of the SBA is the lack of knowledge about what happens to the firms it helps. As discussed, its measures of success are based on the number of loans approved, not the outcome for the firm. The Urban Institute's study was revealing, but even then, there has been no investigation into what would have happened to the SBA-aided firms if the agency had not intervened and no loan was granted. KfW also provides very little information about the exact uses of its loans, referring only to the volume of lending: there is no system in place to measure the outcomes its financing produces. Given that the British investment bank would be in regular, intimate contact with the firms it lends to, it would do well to learn from this mistake. It should compile regular reports on the comparative value of its services, so as better to deliver them.

Advice is a two-way process and EB should provide this upwards as well as downwards. The UK has no real equivalent to the SBA's role as a 'voice for small businesses'. While organisations such as the CBI or EEF try to lobby the government on behalf of manufacturers and businesses, they do so from outside government and have to juggle the needs of all their members, meaning that the views of the SMEs sometimes get lost among those of the influential corporations. The US and Germany both receive SME feedback from their state-backed institutions. KfW provides it via its annual *Mittelstandspanel Report* and the SBA does so through the yearly *The Small Business Economy: A Report to the President*. Given its state-owned status and close contact with SMEs, it would be highly beneficial for the EB to report back to the government annually, in an official manner, on the state of SMEs. Knowing the barriers to commercial loans, their demand and their most frequent uses would go a long way to creating a picture of the business climate that is often overlooked by the government.

The EB should also have a role as a consultancy body for the government, being called on to deliver expert opinions on matters affecting UK industry. Given the expert knowledge the EB will develop, it will be the best placed to advise on the impact of changes in the law on a macroeconomic scale. This role has already been seen in the American SBA's Office of Advocacy, which is routinely invited to participate in discussions on regulation and also conducts investigations on its own initiative. Like the Office, it would be good to judge the success of the bank's consultancy work by the quantity of SME money saved for, say, every hundred pounds spent by this wing of the EB. While other factors might influence the shape of legislation, this rough indicator will show whether or not the Bank is listened to by the government and adjustments made accordingly. This active rather than reactive stance is something not really found in the UK and is non-existent at official government levels.

Beyond businesses

Infrastructure is a key area in which the existing market funding fails. There is little to attract investors if, while a project might be profitable in the long run, the short-term risks are too high. Given the wider benefit of modern, efficient infrastructure to the overall economy, there would be a real case for EB involvement. Improved roads, rail links and airports all help businesses and benefit a wide area. Developing these in regions often overlooked by Westminster-based decision makers, such as the North East and North West of England, would be a boon for countless SMEs, and would justify their not inconsequential cost. While the ICFC never involved itself here, that other example of a successful EB, KfW, has been investing in infrastructure since its inception via the subsidiary, KfW-Kommunalbank (KfW Municipal Bank). Loans totalling €847 million were extended for German infrastructure projects in 2010 alone, including funds from the Infrastructure Investment Offensive which formed part of the Federal Government's economic stimulus packages following the 2008 financial crisis.[4] For example, KfW financed €1.5 million in 2010 to modernise the street lighting in the city of Langen. The modernisation is expected to save €95,000 in energy consumption and €60,000 in street lighting maintenance per year, as well as an annual 467 tonne reduction in CO_2 emissions.[5]

The development of energy supplies in particular is often left short of funding. Given its often long-term nature, it is hard to persuade investors looking for a quick return to involve themselves. This is especially true for nuclear power (which has huge capital costs) and the most promising forms of pre-commercialised low-carbon power (such as marine systems, *not* wind). For example, a £3.5 billion scheme mooted for the Mersey Estuary was cancelled, and according to the assessors of the project, Peel Energy, this was because:

> In the longer term, once the upfront capital costs have been paid off and for the rest of its 120 year life, the cost of electricity would be very competitive. But the preferred scheme is unlikely to attract the necessary investment while the emphasis in the financial sector and renewable energy incentives is on technologies that provide short to medium term returns.[6]

The high R&D costs mean that, without help, this technology is unlikely to get off the ground. Similarly, nuclear power is no longer to receive any government subsidies, at least in theory. Given how pressing our energy security is, with up to a quarter of the UK's power supplies shutting down by 2016, ending subsidies means alternative funds have to be found fast. Here, the EB could step in, alongside conventional private sector investment. Keeping the lights on, via low-cost low-carbon nuclear power, is clearly a public good.

Investing in projects 'for the public good' does not fly the face of the EB's necessary prime aim of making a return on investments. The aim will always be to see a profit on lending, but the timescale on which this occurs is irrelevant. The whole point is to move away from the emphasis on short-term revenue. However, 'public good' is a very loose term, and could be interpreted in any number of ways by the Bank. It would perhaps be best to reduce the scope of interpretation by defining extra-business investments as acceptable only when 'delivering long-term benefit to the economy and wider society for the lowest opportunity cost'. For example, it would be unwise for the Bank to invest £X billion in offshore wind turbines (19p/kWh), if the same investment in nuclear power (10p/kWh) will produce nearly twice as much power for the same cost.[7] Using this sort of critique depoliticises the decision-making, which streamlines an otherwise fraught process still too often choked by backroom deals and favours in local and national government.

6

How the Enterprise Bank Should Operate

The EB's relationship with commercial lenders

The ICFC and SBA present very different approaches in their relationships with commercial banks. The former was simultaneously funded by and competed with these institutions, while the latter is approached as a 'last resort' if other banks fail to provide. With the former approach, the EB would act as a replacement for existing lenders, providing credit to firms regardless of their ability to obtain it from the commercial banks. This could lead to a situation where the private market decides to withdraw from SME lending altogether, on the basis that competing to provide loans by shaving interest rates will lead to smaller profits that fail to make the investments worthwhile. As a result, this could mean the EB is forced to fill the equity gap on its own, making its job all the harder. This is not a desirable outcome. Conversely, the second approach is too accommodating of private lenders' needs, as without the middleman of a bank, SBA funding is still inaccessible to worthy lenders and there is little the SBA can do to overcome unwillingness.

The optimum approach would be a two-tier method that takes into account both SMEs' and banks' needs while also balancing the risks of failing to alter the *status quo* and crowding out commercial lenders. This is possible through requiring EB loan applicants to apply through a commercial bank initially, and then directly to the EB if unsuccessful. In the first instance, the bank is a middleman through which the EB money flows. It has the prerogative to decide whether to accept the applicant or not, based on the usual measure of creditworthiness and other criteria. If it is decided that the applicant is worthy of the loan, then the bank contacts the EB and additional checks are run by the EB to scrutinise the company. Giving advice benefits the banks: they are more sure of investments and are less likely to see them fail. Given that they do not pay for it either, this is a bonus to cooperating with the EB, gaining a free audit of their investments. After this, the EB arranges for the money to be placed in the borrower's account at the private bank. When paying back the loan instalments, the borrower will pay the commercial bank, which in turn repays it to the EB. This is the most sensible approach as it works with the existing frameworks of the financial institutions that already exist. With commercial bank intermediates, there is no need for either the EB or the borrower to go through process of having to set up new bank accounts and the time and money wasted on such administration is saved.

The risk of the loan will be borne in the main part by the EB, but it would be overly generous to spare the commercial middleman any risk at all. Similarly, the borrowers must remain accountable for their success or failure, so should share some of the risk. While the levels might change according to the details of the loan, it would be sensible for the EB to guarantee something like 80 per cent of the loan, while the commercial lender and borrower assume ten per cent of the credit risk each. This way, everyone has a reason to ensure nothing goes wrong, but it is not great enough to scare off the intermediaries or stop borrowers from accessing the loans.

In return for acting as the intermediary, the commercial bank receives a fee from the EB. The size of this fee should be large enough to exist as an incentive and ensure the banks' willingness to act as the go-between. By offering a fee rather than a cut of the interest rate profits, this allows the loan to be offered at the lowest commercial rates possible so that while it delivers a small profit to the EB, it is still advantageous to the SME. In addition, this means that companies can be assessed on a case-by-case basis, rather than offered a flat interest rate. The EB offers the lowest interest rate it can, and this has no effect on the fee the commercial bank receives, which remains the same, regardless of how safe or risky the borrowing company is. The main issue that arises here is the risk that the private lender decides to reject all non-EB loan applications from SMEs, on the basis that collecting the fees from EB loans is more profitable. In other words, it could incentivise the private lenders to quit the market. This is a serious issue that the EB would have to police. It might be possible for a quota on the ratio of EB to non-EB SME loans to be set.

If the commercial bank refuses to grant an EB loan to the borrower, then it would be possible for the borrower to approach the Enterprise Bank directly. If this occurs, the EB will conduct its own scrutiny of the company, to ensure that it was not rejected simply on the grounds of not being a viable business. It would also take into account other factors that might scare a commercial lender, such as whether the firm is a start-up and the riskiness of the sector it is in. If the borrower appears to have great potential despite these hurdles, then it should still offer a loan, while taking the risk into account when negotiating the interest rate. In this case, the borrower would receive the money and then repay it directly to the

HOW THE ENTERPRISE BANK SHOULD OPERATE

EB. The EB must be able to deal directly with customers if other banks are not, and so it should be seen as just as much of a bank as the other financial institutions. It is only if the government takes the EB seriously that others, including private investors, will follow their lead and do likewise. The end result should be that if the commercial lenders are complacent and do nothing, the EB will become the first port of call for businesses seeking finance.

This two-tier approach does not happen in the KfW lending system, but then there is less need for it there: Britain does not have the same level of bank competition that Germany does. With KfW, the bank is allowed to charge the borrower a fee and a credit margin within a framework set by KfW. The banks need less of an incentive given that there are numerous local and national banks competing for customers' services, so if one bank refuses to grant a KfW loan, there are many more that are highly likely to offer one if the firm is creditworthy. In Britain, the domination of the lending sector by a small number of large banks means it is far more likely that good applicants may be overlooked.

Nonetheless, this approach does ensure that there is no crowding out of private lending, which is the usual criticism of state-backed banks. KfW's record has shown that the crowding out argument is a weak one. By using commercial banks as a distribution channel, its negative effects are minimised. The services KfW offers through direct application are ones that would not usually be offered by the private sector anyway, such as financing for energy efficient modernisation and specific technological innovations. Also, because KfW is financed primarily by its activity on the capital markets, and not through government funding (except where it is charged with administering the government's economic policies e.g. the stimulus packages), its lending doesn't impact too much on government borrowing and consequently interest rates.[1]

As previously noted, the real challenge of filling the equity gap is not getting the state to do this, but the private sector. This means giving banks the breathing space to be able to offer loans without the EB. The private bank will still be entirely at liberty to lend to any comers, and could continue to offer loans as now, independent of the EB, with the funding coming solely from the commercial bank and the profit returning to it. If they decide they would not be willing to do this, the potential borrower should be free to apply for an EB loan from any of the commercial banks, whether they were a previous customer or not. This means that the banks will be more predisposed to help, as they would risk losing an existing customer's patronage. Rather than crowding out, this ensures a healthy level of competition between the commercial lenders. The SBA style of cooperation is therefore not appropriate. Knowing that it cannot act independently, the commercial banks do not feel threatened enough to fill the equity gap of their own accord.

Similarly, if the bank is simply not interested in lending to the applicant, then there is no crowding out there either, as the direct application of an SME to the EB will be as a last resort, after the private market has abandoned them, not before. The addition of the EB to the equation is simply to increase the volume of lending available and to enhance the private market, not replace it.

Which firms would it invest in?

The EB should attempt to lend to the best businesses it finds and use its expertise to accelerate their growth,

HOW THE ENTERPRISE BANK SHOULD OPERATE

bringing it larger returns on investments and therefore supplying it with more funds to invest elsewhere. However, if the EB focuses on filling the equity gap for the SME elite, then many less stellar firms could face a continued funding crisis. Alternatively, the EB could work through the banks to lend to commercial outcasts, potentially ensuring the survival of some and the renaissance of a select few. It could then rely on the private sector seizing the opportunity of investing in the best SMEs without its help.

The choice is a tough one, but when push comes to shove, the EB is not about making sweeping generalisations by investing in some sectors and not others, as is the case in the private market. Instead it is designed to invest on a 'case-by-case' basis, assessing individual firms not just on their creditworthiness, but also on how they fit into the EB's paramount aim of improving the UK economy and balance of trade.

How it should be created

The easiest way to set up the Enterprise Bank would be to use an existing state-owned financial institution that has experience of lending and companies/other banks are used to dealing with. One such institution exists: the Royal Bank of Scotland (RBS). This already has an experienced staff and infrastructure which could be redeployed in aid of SMEs.

The government became a majority shareholder in RBS in November 2008, when it took a 58 per cent stake in the bank. This was increased to 70 per cent in April 2009 and 84 per cent by November 2009, with a total shareholding value of £45 billion, a sum larger than most state departmental annual budgets.

The state ownership of RBS is claimed to be a short-term situation and that it will be sold on as soon as a lucrative deal comes along that will allow the government to recoup the taxpayers' money invested in the bank. However, if UKFI wants to maximise the value of the bank to the taxpayer, there is no reason this could not be done without selling the bank, and keeping it running for long-term value via turning RBS into the Enterprise Bank. If the government is as preoccupied with short-term shareholder value as the private financial sector already is, the equity gap will never be fixed: RBS being kept as just another commercial bank means current weaknesses in the financial system are left unfixed.

RBS already deals with around a quarter of the UK's SMEs, so is ideally placed for the transformation as it means it must already have relationships with many companies and an understanding of how they work.[2] Additionally, many RBS staff will be trained in industrial lending, so there will be no need to poach employees from other banks and generate ill-will. It also has a country-wide network of bank branches which, while not specialised for SMEs at the moment, would lend nicely to becoming such hubs in the areas that they are needed. In all, RBS is a working bank with all the necessary components required for the EB, all it needs is a change of focus.

The form of the Enterprise Bank

By its nature, the Enterprise Bank would necessitate a return to a more personalised banking mechanism where managers and customers know each other. Simply accepting or rejecting clients based on credit scores and inflexible criteria would be contradictory to the purpose of its operation.

HOW THE ENTERPRISE BANK SHOULD OPERATE

It goes without saying that the bank would need to be independent of party political pressure, but this does not mean that it will also be unaccountable. Given that it exists to serve the public interest, while day-to-day decisions should not be subjected to political scrutiny, the overall investment portfolio could be. KfW was given certain goals such as financing the improvement of domestic production and exports and achieved these: the financing volume in this area increased from DM 106 million to DM 1 billion between the mid-1950s and 1960s. It grew further, more than fivefold, between the 1970s and 1980s, reaching €59.8 billion in 2010. In 2011 KfW IPEX-Bank provided, along with investments from five other banks, a buyer loan of €390 million to an Indian company constructing a gas and steam power plant in Singapore to ensure the export of German high technology: the turbines at the centre of the plant are constructed in Germany by Siemens. The energy-efficient nature of the project is a further benefit in the eyes of KfW IPEX-Bank.[3] The aims simultaneously allow great scope for interpretation but are also very clear in their intentions. By looking at this wider picture, if it is felt that the Bank is putting profit before any other motive, there would certainly be reason to call its executive to account and require justification for the decisions made.

This privilege should not be used lightly and the precedent of the most government-overseen bank supports this. As stated earlier, KfW is overseen by a Supervisory Board, which itself is headed by the German Federal Minister for Finance, presently Dr Wolfgang Schäuble. All the other Supervisory Board members are in some way or another political appointments as well. Additionally, KfW has a dedicated SME Advisory Council. Its role is defined:

The Mittelstandsrat (SME Advisory Council) specifies the state mandate of KfW Mittelstandsbank. It deliberates and takes decisions on proposals for the promotion of small- and medium-sized enterprises, taking into consideration the overall business planning of the Institution.[4]

The members of this council are also politicians. However, the intervention of the Supervisory Board and SME Council beyond general decision making is rare. That said, this is not necessarily a good thing: as the reaction of the supervisory board to the Lehman Brothers debacle showed, little was done to investigate how such an erroneous decision (making the auto-payment) was taken. It was not in the interests of the politicians to scrutinise their own failings in the bank, given these would have repercussions on their elective ability. For them, it was better to bury their heads in the sand and forget about the whole issue. This would suggest that a political supervisory board for the EB would be pointless, useful for little more than rubber-stamping decisions. As such, the EB should be headed by a committee similar to the ICFC's in design, composed of very experienced industrialists and a few bankers, with real power. If a scrutinising body is felt to be required, this should have no vested interest in hiding the failings of the Bank and should be free from political influence that could otherwise press a certain line on it.

The EB is not a commercial bank, and therefore its remuneration packages should reflect this. The fast-living bonus culture has no place whatsoever in an organisation that seeks to invest in the long-term, where short-termism would be a liability, not an asset. The standard practise of rewarding maximisation of profits with bonuses does not sit well with this 'slow cooking'. Having said that, there are many competent and knowledgeable bankers at existing institutions who would be real assets to the EB. These men and women would like to invest for the long-term and with their borrowers' interests in mind, but for the most part, they are severely constrained in their current jobs. The EB could offer a way out for them. Perhaps the solution would be to offer attractive salaries but without the expectation of bonuses as a right rather than a privilege.

Where should it be based

At the very least, the EB should not be located in the City of London. The whole point of the neo-ICFC would be to retain the two key essences of the original institution: the industrial expertise and the intimate relationships with individual companies. Neither of these aims could be served by basing the Bank in London which is almost as far from most manufacturers as possible in the UK. Instead, the Bank will necessarily have a very decentralised organisation, with regional branches located in the cities of the industrial areas. The head office should be centred similarly, perhaps in Newcastle or Middlesbrough. Given the EB would be operating partially through existing banks, there would not be a need for too many EB branches. KfW for example has offices in just three German cities since the majority of its financing comes through banks with branches in every town across the country. Similarly, KfW's close cooperation with the eighteen promotional banks in the federal states of Germany means that a direct link to KfW is never too far away.

A certain level of autonomy would be absolutely vital to the EB branches as their makeup and portfolio weighting would have to reflect regional emphases: an investment that would make sense in Sheffield might appear more risky if it were made in Carlisle. Similarly, the experts in the Bank would vary in terms of specialisation according to the area, so that the local factors could be taken into account during decision making. This approach would be much more effective than simply having a central Bank from which, say, an electronics industry expert would be dispatched to assess a microprocessor manufacturer's business. While the expert might be able to scrutinise any electronics firm in the country, by concentrating on the bigger picture, they might overlook crucial local conditions that should make or break the decision. In addition, they could not use their indigenous knowledge to identify up-and-coming companies and actively approach them. Far better then that the Bank becomes a hydra, with the central body merely acting as the holder of the purse strings and regulator.

How success should be measured

The problem with other state-backed investment institutions has often been the lack of tangible measures of success. The SBA judges its work on the basis of the volume of money given out and the number of loans they provide, while KfW relies solely on the former. While measures of output such as these are useful to show the level of activity and the extent of these institutions' involvement in the economy, they do not actually provide a real indication of the impact the investments are having. For this, measures of outcome are needed, which are the only way to ensure the goals of the organisation are really being reached. By default, many of the companies that these national investment institutions are lending to are likely to be less stable than average due to being start-ups, at a turning point of capital growth or other vulnerable points in a business's evolution. These factors, plus long-term economic conditions and other influences, mean there are many variables other than the loan that have a significant impact on the business's ability. Without measures of outcome, the extent to which the loan is the difference between success and failure is impossible to gauge.

While measuring this is hard, it is not impossible. Outcome could be assessed through examining how companies perform after receiving a loan, such as the number of new employees hired or how many other investments it secures. Despite having been told to shift to these measures by the US Government Accountability Office, the SBA has not yet completed the transition, and indeed it might never do so due to 'the costs and legal concerns associated with obtaining the necessary information to undertake this impact analysis'.[5] If access to such information were a pre-requisite to receiving an investment from the EB, this would be overcome before it even became an issue.

It is vital that the EB's impact is clear, and not just for issues of transparency associated with spending taxpayers' money. The Bank would need to know the true extent of its success, to allow it better to tailor its services to businesses and so that these firms know whether the EB loan is the best investment they can obtain if others are also available. If, as would be expected, the EB is successful in meeting its goals in terms of measure of outcome, then demand for its services would probably increase.

EU state aid issues

With the EB using state resources, along with private capital, the bank will need to abide by EU state-aid rules, although this does not mean that its investment decisions need to be constrained in any significant way. The European Union's rules on state-aid, as outlined in Article 107 of the Treaty of the Functioning of the European Union (TFEU), seek to prevent governments using public resources to distort the European single market. Nevertheless, the rules are filled with exemptions which allow distortions where the wider benefits of the aid measure are greater than the negative effect upon competition. Furthermore, public investment is allowed where it is demonstrated that an investment has been made in accordance with the 'market economy investor principle' (MEIP). The MEIP is a test of whether a public investment mirrors that which could, or would, be made by a private investor operating in a well-functioning market.

Recent market interventions by KfW demonstrate how the Enterprise Bank could satisfy EU rules. Following the financial crisis and ensuing recession, KfW acted to support German businesses. In 2010, the European Commission gave its approval to €78 million worth of lending by KfW to protect jobs at German firms and there were no restrictions on the firms receiving aid. That said, the Commission gave its approval on the understanding that loans would meet the requirements of the MEIP. A British state-backed bank would have to ensure that any investments it made met the requirements of the MEIP but it could also provide finance to businesses on terms more favourable than those found in the market if such aid served objectives approved by the Commission. There are also exemptions covering aid for research, development and innovation, aid for training, aid of a social character, aid provided as a response to natural disasters or exceptional circumstances, aid for cultural purposes, aid to address regional economic underdevelopment and aid that helps execute a project of common European interest. The breadth of these exemptions gives governments or disbursers of public funds significant scope to support individual sectors or firms. A general industry bank would be able to take advantage of this.

This is not to say the EB will not have to be careful. In 2002, KfW had to make one of its subsidiaries, KfW IPEX-Bank, legally independent as its financing activities were deemed by the European Commission to be in direct competition with the private sector: ongoing support for these activities from the Federal Government would be considered in contravention of the state-aid rules. On 1 January 2008, KfW IPEX-Bank became independent, which means it no longer benefits from Federal Government guarantees and support.[6] Given the EB will be working through commercial banks where possible, it should avoid falling foul of this.

7

How the Enterprise Bank Should Be Funded

The most important thing, when considering how to fund the EB, is to learn from the mistakes of the ICFC. Generating funds through the selling of stock was sipping from the devil's cup, and as the first part of this report showed, it led to the demise of its public service role. It would be better if the EB's funds were smaller than they could otherwise be, if this guarantees the independence and long-term nature of its investments.

Given that the Green Investment Bank will be receiving £3 billion in start-up funds, the Enterprise Bank should expect to receive at least an equal sum. Indeed, given the former's narrow remit, the EB should be granted more, as an acknowledgement of its wider role in the economy. After the initial injection of state money, the next step is to get around the tricky question of how to raise non-governmental funds to maximise the Bank's impact. It would perhaps be best to look to the private capital market. Research conducted by Robert Skidelsky and Felix Martin has used the example of the European Investment Bank to show that on an initial outlay of €50 billion, the EIB secured an additional €420 billion.[1] If this ratio of 1:8.4 stands true for the EB, then an initial £3 billion could raise roughly another £25 billion, making a not-insignificant grand total of £28 billion to invest as necessary.

HOW THE ENTERPRISE BANK SHOULD BE FUNDED

It might appear obvious, but the EB should be explicitly backed by the government, to ensure that it will not fail. Given that the EB does intend to make a return on its loans, while also be lending as cheaply as possible, the only way to balance this is to ensure that the bank itself can borrow at the lowest rate, below those offered to non-guaranteed banks. The government backing is entirely necessary for this, to ensure that, when leveraging private funds, the bank is deemed entirely safe and can therefore access the cheapest credit available to it, *à la* KfW.

A decision must be made on how the EB invests. Ensuring that ventures are commercially sound and unlikely to fail does not mean that all loans given out will prove to have a significant effect on the economy. In addition, decisions will have to be made on where the balance lies between granting emergency loans to existing, successful companies to ensure their continued existence and providing funds to high-risk high-reward firms that have great potential. Looking at the examples used, it would appear that, in terms of loans, the ICFC was a more commercial organisation than the SBA. While both have a record of rejecting bad applicants, the former, at least initially, relied on the revenues raised from its loans to be able to provide further ones, so getting the maximum return on a less-than-commercially-desirable loan was challenging but achievable. The SBA, receiving half of its funding from federal revenues, has less of an impetus to invest in this way as national interest, rather than ensuring returns, is the prerogative. How then should the EB run? Assuming it would not be receiving continuous government funding once initialised, it would have to lend with its self-preservation in mind. However, this must not lead to the profit-driven lending practises of other banks. If it were enshrined in law that all profit the

EB made was automatically reallocated for investment in other companies, the EB would have the greatest possible effect on the economy. By mixing its portfolio, using some steady loans to failsafe companies, these could be used to offset the chances taken on high-risk high-return ones.

There are numerous routes the government could take to find funding for the Enterprise Bank. The creation of the institution from publicly-owned RBS has already been discussed, and this would in itself be a source of initial funding. With an annual revenue of £30 billion, and assets of over £1.4 trillion, many of which could be sold off, this is one of the greatest funding mechanisms the government could use.[2] It is not the intention of this report to go into detail about how or which of these potential solutions should be used, for fear of vastly over-simplifying the issues: each would likely merit a detailed report in its own right. Instead, the following 'food for thought' bullet points should suffice:

- Given the huge sums of money being injected indirectly into the financial markets via quantitative easing (QE), earmarking some of this for redirection into founding the EB would mean the lending crisis QE aims to solve indirectly could be tackled head on. This would not be a particularly tricky thing to do. At present, the Bank of England creates money via QE to buy government bonds off commercial banks, in the hope that their increased liquidity will mean they provide more loans to individuals and businesses, but has no control over ensuring this. Instead, if the Enterprise Bank sold its own bonds, then the Bank of England could purchase these instead, providing the EB with the money it would require to increase its lending. This would directly ensure QE achieves its goal, rather than leaving it to chance and cooperation. This would also mean that the taxpayer is not having to fund the EB.

- The government could pressure the commercial banks to plough some of their money into the EB's creation, as with the setting up of the ICFC and Big Society Capital.

- As a short-term solution while waiting for the EB to open, the government should improve SME lending by providing backing to loans made by commercial banks.

- Alternatively, it could lower the amount of capital banks require to back loans, to allow them to grant more. Both of these latter suggestions, if passed straight away, would have an immediate effect and rapidly ameliorate conditions for those creditworthy companies suffering from credit rationing.

The EB is intended to be an institution that will serve the UK now, in the good times to come, and in future crises. Once set up, it would act as a channel through which quantitative easing could be delivered. Much like the SBA, which had increased funds injected into it in the wake of the recession, the EB could be granted more money via QE when it is necessary to get more lending to SMEs and this funding could then be reduced after the storm has passed. In this way, it would become a formal aspect of monetary policy and another tool for the Bank of England to use.

Another important point to consider is the cost to the taxpayer. It is more challenging for politicians to push through the Bank's creation if it will cost the taxpayer money, year in, year out. This is not necessarily a problem. Given that there has been no real public disapproval of the GIB's £3 billion foundation, courtesy of the taxpayer, it is unlikely the EB would face any significant opposition either, especially since it will deliver more jobs and have a larger impact than the GIB could ever hope to. Indeed, the EB will be an investment of public funds, as the growth in jobs and revenue it brings will see larger returns to the Treasury in time. Rather than being concerned about the EB spending taxpayers' money, we should be delighted that it does. Regardless, the EB could be founded on taxpayers' money at its inception but then left to fund itself through returns on its investment, gradually building up a sizable portfolio and multiplying its returns. At a basic level, this is what KfW has done, and most of its current assets can be traced back to money provided out of the original Marshal Plan funds. As such, the discussion about spending taxpayers' money could be rendered moot, and politicians would therefore have nothing to fear by creating it.

8

Conclusion

The efforts expended so far on trying to alleviate the funding shortages in various sectors of the economy give an indication that the government *is* aware of the problems businesses face in trying to secure loans. At the same time though, their efforts may be too little and too late. With the financial crisis probably continuing to loom over Britain for the next few years and, in all likelihood, getting worse, there has never been a better time to perform major surgery on the lending system. It is also possible to look at this from the other side, and the urgency of the issue becomes apparent: without any significant change to our current system, the collapse of vast swathes of SMEs and, as a consequence, the British economy is highly plausible.

The Enterprise Bank offers the UK two solutions to this perhaps inevitable downturn. Firstly, it alleviates the problems many firms are already facing. Secondly, it improves the general business environment, making Britain more attractive for businesses to set up shop. This will have a long-term benefit as spin-offs or other start-ups, that otherwise could not find the means to base themselves in the UK, will no longer have to move abroad. At present, we are losing many businesses every year because of this, leading to fewer jobs and lower export rates. Obviously, the Enterprise Bank is not a 'magic bullet' that can allay all our economic woes, but it is a great place to start and will ensure that whenever the next financial crisis occurs, Britain will be in a much stronger position to surmount it.

Notes

Foreword

1. Vickers, Sir John, *Final Report Recommendations, Independent Commission on Banking*, September 2011, p. 16; http://bankingcommission.s3.amazonaws.com/wp-content/uploads/2010/07/ICB-Final-Report.pdf
2. *Independent Commission on Banking*, p. 15.
3. *Independent Commission on Banking*, p. 153.
4. *Future of Banking Commission* (FBC), 2010, p. 58; http://commission.bnbb.org/banking/sites/all/themes/whichfobtheme/pdf/commission_report.pdf
5. FBC, p. 59.
6. FBC, p. 59.
7. FBC, p. 66.

1: The Industrial and Commercial Finance Corporation

1. Quoted in: Radcliffe Committee on the Working of the Monetary system (para. 937), 1959.
2. Murphy, G.W. & Prusmann, D., 'The Industrial and Commercial Finance Corporation – A Progress Report', *The Manchester School*, vol. 36 (3), September 1968, p. 226.
3. Coopey, R. & Clarke, D., *Fifty Years Investing in Industry*, 1995, p. 376.
4. Lonsdale, C., *The UK Equity Gap: the failure of government policy since 1945*, 1997, p. 40.
5. Murthy, R.V., 'The UK's New Financial Corporations: FCI and ICFC', in Agarwala, A.N. (ed.), *Public Corporations: an expert study*, 1945, p. 59.

6 Tew, B., 'The I.C.F.C. Revisited', *Economica,* vol. 22 (87), August 1955, p. 225.

7 Murphy & Prusmann, 'The Industrial and Commercial Finance Corporation', p. 230

8 Corporate Direction International, *The Finance of Small and Medium Sized Businesses*, 1961, p. 25.

9 Murphy & Prusmann, 'The Industrial and Commercial Finance Corporation', p. 235.

10 The table on p. 236 of Murphy & Prusmann gives a full breakdown by region and industry sector at 31 March 1967.

11 Coopey, R., 'The First Venture Capitalist: Financing Development in Britain After 1945, The Case of ICFC/3i', *Business and Economic History,* vol. 23 (1), Fall 1994, p. 265.

12 Ross, D.M., *The Clearing Banks and the Finance of British Industry, 1930-58,* 1990, p. 6.

13 C.D. International, *The Finance of Small and Medium Sized Businesses*, p. 8.

14 Murphy & Prusmann, 'The Industrial and Commercial Finance Corporation', p. 232.

15 Ross, *The Clearing Banks and the Finance of British Industry, 1930-58*, p. 8.

16 Radcliffe Committee on the Working of the Monetary system (para. 945).

17 Ross, *The Clearing Banks and the Finance of British Industry, 1930-58*, p. 8.

18 C.D. International, *The Finance of Small and Medium Sized Businesses*, p. 18.

19 Tew, 'The I.C.F.C. Revisited', p. 218.

20 Coopey, 'The First Venture Capitalist', p. 265.

NOTES

21 Murphy & Prusmann, 'The Industrial and Commercial Finance Corporation', p. 225.

22 Murphy & Prusmann, 'The Industrial and Commercial Finance Corporation', p. 238.

23 Tew, 'The I.C.F.C. Revisited', p. 232.

24 Coopey, 'The First Venture Capitalist', p. 267.

25 Coopey, 'The First Venture Capitalist', p. 267.

26 Coopey & Clarke, *Fifty Years Investing in Industry*, p. 114.

27 Coopey & Clarke, *Fifty Years Investing in Industry*, p. 115.

28 Coopey, 'The First Venture Capitalist', p. 269.

29 Coopey & Clarke, *Fifty Years Investing in Industry*, p. 87.

30 Coopey & Clarke, *Fifty Years Investing in Industry*, p. 87.

31 C.D. International, *The Finance of Small and Medium sized Businesses*, p. 11.

32 C.D. International, *The Finance of Small and Medium sized Businesses*, p. 13.

33 C.D. International, *The Finance of Small and Medium sized Businesses*, p. 73.

34 Tew, 'The I.C.F.C. Revisited', p. 222.

35 Tew, 'The I.C.F.C. Revisited', p. 229.

36 Coopey & Clarke, *Fifty Years Investing in Industry*, p. 376.

37 Macmillan Committee on Finance & Industry (para. 404), 1931.

38 Murphy & Prusmann, 'The Industrial and Commercial Finance Corporation', p. 236.

39 Anglo-German Foundation for the Study of Industrial Society, *Small and Medium Sized Enterprise Financing in the UK: lessons from Germany*, 1994, p. 2.

40 http://www.bis.gov.uk/policies/enterprise-and-business-support/access-to-finance/enterprise-finance-guarantee

41 Macmillan Committee on Finance & Industry (para. 403).

2: The US Small Business Administration

1 http://web.sba.gov/faqs/faqindex.cfm?areaID=24 (Q.1 *What is a Small Business*).

2 http://www.sba.gov/sites/default/files/sbfaq.pdf

3 http://smallbusiness.com/wiki/Small-Business_Administration

4 http://smallbusiness.com/wiki/Small-Business_Administration

5 US Small Business Administration, *FY2012 Congressional Budget Justification and FY2010 Annual Performance Report*, p. 1.

6 http://www.sba.gov/about-offices-content/2/3107/success-stories

7 *FY2012 Congressional Budget Justification*, p. 32.

8 The Urban Institute, *An Assessment of Small Business Loan and Investment Performance: Survey of Assisted Businesses*, January 2008, p. 2.

9 http://www.sba.gov/about-offices-content/2/3159/success-stories/4098

10 http://www.sba.gov/content/export-loan-programs#Export%20Working%20Capital%20Program%20%28EWCP%29

NOTES

11 http://www.sba.gov/sites/default/files/ ITL%20small%20business.pdf

12 *FY2012 Congressional Budget Justification*, p. 24.

13 http://www.sba.gov/content/cdc504-loan-program

14 http://www.sba.gov/about-offices-content/1/2890/about-us

15 http://www.smallbusinessnotes.com/business-finances/small-business-investment-companies-sbics.html#b

16 http://www.sba.gov/content/sbic-application-process

17 http://www.smallbusinessnotes.com/business-finances/small-business-investment-companies-sbics.html#b

18 http://www.sbaonline.sba.gov/idc/groups/public/ documents/sba_homepage/news_release_10-60.pdf

19 Urban Institute, *Key Findings from the Evaluation of the Small Business Administration's Loan and Investment Programs: Executive Summary*, January 2008, p. 2.

20 *Key Findings*, p. 8.

21 *Key Findings*, p. 11.

22 *Key Findings*, p. 27.

23 *Key Findings*, p. 42.

24 *FY2012 Congressional Budget Justification*, p. 1.

25 *FY2012 Congressional Budget Justification*, p. 31.

26 *FY2012 Congressional Budget Justification*, p. 31.

27 *FY2012 Congressional Budget Justification*, p. 32.

28 US Government Accountability Office, *Small Business Administration: operations and programs*, New York, 2008, p. 25.

29 *Small Business Administration: operations and programs*, pp. 2 & 64.

30 *Small Business Administration: operations and programs*, p. 65.

31 *Small Business Administration: operations and programs*, p. 29.

32 The Urban Institute, *Key Findings From the Evaluation of the Small Business Administration's Loan and Investment Programs: Executive Summary*, January 2008, pp. 10-11.

33 The Urban Institute, *Competitive and Special Competitive Opportunity Gap Analysis of the 7(a) and 504 Programs*, January 2008, pp. 10-18.

34 The Urban Institute, *An Assessment of Small Business Loan and Investment Performance*, p. 5.

35 *An Assessment of Small Business Loan and Investment Performance*, p. 5.

36 *Small Business Administration: operations and programs*, p. 25.

37 The Urban Institute, *An Assessment of Small Business Loan and Investment Performance*, p. 4.

38 *Small Business Administration: operations and programs*, p. 31.

39 *FY2012 Congressional Budget Justification*, p. 22.

40 *FY2012 Congressional Budget Justification*, p. 108.

41 http://www.sba.gov/advocacy/816/25801

42 *FY2012 Congressional Budget Justification*, p. 108.

43 http://www.score.org/

44 http://www.score.org/our-impact

45 *FY2012 Congressional Budget Justification*, p. 48.

46 SCORE, *FY2009 Annual Report*, p. 13.

47 *FY2012 Congressional Budget Justification*, p. 34.

NOTES

48 *FY2012 Congressional Budget Justification*, p. 33 & 36.

49 *FY2012 Congressional Budget Justification*, p. 33 & 36.

50 *Small Business Administration: operations and programs*, p. 13.

51 *FY2012 Congressional Budget Justification*, p. 32.

52 'SBA-Backed Loans Dry Up at Crucial Time for Businesses', *Wall Street Journal*, 4 November 2008.

53 'SBA-Backed Loans Dry Up at Crucial Time for Businesses' & *FY2012 Congressional Budget Justification*, p. 33 & 36.

54 *Small Business Administration: operations and programs*, p. 2.

55 http://www.newrules.org/news/chart-number-banks-us-19662008

56 http://www.standardandpoors.com/products-services/articles/en/us/?assetID=1245225768756, Chart 3.

57 http://www.businessweek.com/debateroom/archives/2007/06/axe_the_sba.html

58 Coleman, B., *The Coleman Report: The SBA Lender's Industry Information Source*, June 2011, p. 1.

59 US Census Bureau, *Statistics of US Businesses: US All Industries*.

60 *Small Business Administration: operations and programs*, p. 25.

61 *Small Business Administration: operations and programs*, p. 66.

62 The Urban Institute, *An Assessment of Small Business Loan and Investment Performance*, p. 5.

3: KfW

1 KfW Bankengruppe, *Annual Report 2010*, (2011) p. i.

2 *Global Finance*, 'World's Fifty Safest Banks 2011', 18 August 2011.

3 *Annual Report 2010*, p. 9.

4 *Annual Report 2010*, p. 56.

5 Grünbacher, A., 'The Early Years of a German Institution: the Kreditanstalt für Wiederaufbau in the 1950s', *Business History* 43, (4), 2001, p. 71.

6 *Annual Report 2010*, pp. 130-31.

7 Grünbacher, A., *Reconstruction and Cold War in Germany: The Kreditanstalt für Wideraufbau (1948-1961)*, Ashgate, 2004, p. 262.

8 Grünbacher, 'The Early Years of a German Institution', p. 71.

9 'The Early Years of a German Institution', pp. 72-73 & 78.

10 KfW Bankengruppe, *History of KfW: From the Kreditanstalt für Wiederaufbau to the KfW Bankengruppe*.

11 Grünbacher, 'The Early Years of a German Institution, p. 78.

12 *History of KfW*.

13 Grünbacher, 'The Early Years of a German Institution', p. 76.

14 Harries, H., *Financing the Future: KfW – the German Bank with a Public Mission*, Frankfurt am Main, 1998, p. 41.

15 *Financing the Future*, p. 42.

16 Grünbacher, 'The Early Years of a German Institution', p. 79.

17 *Funding Universe*, 'Company History and Profiles: Kreditanstalt für Wiederaufbau'.

18 Grünbacher, 'The Early Years of a German Institution', p. 75.

19 'The Early Years of a German Institution', pp. 76-77.

20 KfW Bankengruppe, *Facts and Figures: KfW – An Overview*, April 2011 p. 18.

21 *Facts and Figures: KfW – An Overview*, pp. 4-6.

NOTES

22 *History of KfW.*

23 *Funding Universe*, 'Company History and Profiles: Kreditanstalt für Wiederaufbau'.

24 Harries, *Financing the Future*, p. 57.

25 Grünbacher, *Reconstruction and Cold War in Germany*, pp. 260-61.

26 *Annual Report 2010*, p. 8.

27 KfW Bankengruppe, *Facts and Figures: KfW – An Overview*, p. 19.

28 Harries, *Financing the Future*, pp.120-21.

29 *History of KfW.*

30 KfW Bankengruppe, *Facts and Figures: KfW – An Overview*, p. 19.

31 *History of KfW.*

32 *Facts and Figures: KfW – An Overview*, p. 19.

33 *History of KfW.*

34 *History of KfW.*

35 *History of KfW.*

36 *History of KfW.*

37 *History of KfW.*

38 Grünbacher, *Reconstruction and Cold War in Germany*, p. 261.

39 Harries, *Financing the Future*, p. 58.

40 *History of KfW.*

41 KfW Bankengruppe, *Facts and Figures: KfW – An Overview*, April 2011 p. 3.

42 KfW Bankengruppe, *Financial Report 2010*, March 2011, p. 70.

43 *History of KfW.*

44 *Annual Report 2010*, p. 47.

45 *History of KfW.*

46 'Home sweet home is a rented property for many Germans: Germany has avoided British-style property market bubbles', *Guardian*, 16 March 2011.

47 'KfW Is Raided Over EU 319 Million Transfer to Lehman', *Bloomberg*, 22 October 2008.

48 'Police raid "Germany's dumbest bank" in Lehman transaction probe', *Guardian*, 23 October 2008.

49 'KfW Is Raided Over EU 319 Million Transfer to Lehman'.

50 'KfW Is Raided Over EU 319 Million Transfer to Lehman'.

51 KfW Bankengruppe, 'Comments by KfW Bankengruppe on article "KfW transfer was apparently intentional"' in *Frankfurter Allgemeine Zeitung* of 22 September 2008, 22 September 2008.

52 KfW Bankengruppe, *KfW Draws Consequences from Lehman Incident*, September 2008.

53 'KfW chiefs may face legal action', *Telegraph*, 21 September 2008.

54 Grünbacher, 'The Early Years of a German Institution', p. 81.

55 *Annual Report 2010*, p. 34.

56 *Annual Report 2010*, p. 9.

57 *Annual Report 2010*, p. 34.

58 Standard & Poor's, *KfW*, September 2009.

59 *Annual Report 2010*, p. 43.

60 *Annual Report 2010*, p. 29.

NOTES

61 KfW Bankengruppe, *How to Apply for a KfW Loan*.

62 KfW Bankengruppe, *KfW Gründungsmonitor 2011*, April 2011, p. 48.

63 *Annual Report 2010*, p. 44.

64 *Annual Report 2010*, p. 45.

65 *How to Apply for a KfW Loan*.

66 *Financial Report 2010*, pp. 104-5.

67 *Annual Report 2010*, p. 34.

68 European Commission, *State aid N 661/2008 – Germany KfW-run Special Programme 2009*, December 2008, p. 25.

69 State aid N 661/2008 – Germany KfW-run Special Programme 2009, p. 22.

70 KfW Bankengruppe, *Beratung in Krisen*.

71 KfW Bankengruppe, *Export Finance*.

72 *Export Finance*.

73 *Financial Report 2010*, p. 72.

74 KfW Bankengruppe, *ERP Export Financing Programme*.

75 *Annual Report 2010*, p. 66.

76 KfW Bankengruppe, *Full Steam Ahead*, p. 1.

77 KfW Bankengruppe, *Financing for Small Exports*.

4: Existing British Institutions Aimed at Alleviating the Macmillan Gap

1 Green Investment Bank Commission, *Unlocking Investment to Deliver Britain's Low Carbon Future*, June 2010, p. xiii.

2 *Unlocking Investment to Deliver Britain's Low Carbon Future*, p. xiii.

3   HM Government, *Update on the Design of the Green Investment Bank*, May 2011, p. 6.

4   *The Autumn Statement 2011*, HM Treasury, p. 38.

5   All from http://www.bis.gov.uk/policies/enterprise-and-business-support/access-to-finance/enterprise-finance-guarantee/efg-statistics

6   http://www.businesszone.co.uk/topic/finances/bis-stats-reveal-enterprise-finance-guarantee-scheme-lending-free-fall/36974

7   http://www.bis.gov.uk/policies/enterprise-and-business-support/access-to-finance/ex-efg

5: What Should the Enterprise Bank Do?

1   ONS, *UK Business: Activity, Size and Location – 2010*, Table A5.3.

2   European Association of Development Agencies, *All Money is Not the Same*, September 2011, p. 14.

3   US Government Accountability Office, *Small Business Administration: Operations and Programs*, New York, 2008, p. 18.

4   KfW Bankengruppe, *Annual Report 2010*, 2011, p. 41.

5   KfW Bankengruppe website, *Förderbeispiel 1*.

6   http://www.bbc.co.uk/news/uk-england-merseyside-13875032

7   http://www.decc.gov.uk/assets/decc/statistics/projections/71-uk-electricity-generation-costs-update-.pdf

6: How the EB Should Operate

1   http://www.ft.com/cms/s/0/f960f190-d6fc-11df-aaab-00144feabdc0.html#axzz1c5R5AHDT

NOTES

2 http://www.wdm.org.uk/sites/default/files/ A%20Bank%20for%20the%20Future.pdf
3 KfW IPEX-Bank, *Energy Efficiency 'made in Germany'*, August 2011.
4 http://k-f-w.org/kfw/en/KfW_Group/About_KfW/Vorstand_und_Gremien/SME_Advisory_Council.jsp
5 US Government Accountability Office, *Small Business Administration: Operations and Programs*, New York, 2008, p. 36.
6 Standard & Poor's, *KfW*, September 2009.

7: How the EB Should Be Funded

1 Skidelsky, R. & Martin, F., 'For a National Investment Bank', *New York Review of Books*, March 2011.
2 http://www.investors.rbs.com/ download/announcements/Announcement_RBS_Annual_Results_2010.pdf